LIFE IN SCOTLAND

Part of the Roman road between Biggar and Edinburgh.

LIFE IN SCOTLAND

from the Stone Age to the Twentieth Century

NORMAN NICHOL

illustrations by Ron Stenberg

Adam & Charles Black · London

The Palace of Holyroodhouse in 1647. It had been built by James IV and his successors who wanted a more comfortable place to live than the fortified Edinburgh Castle.

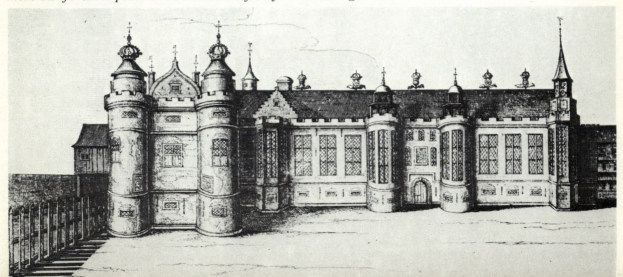

LIFE IN SCOTLAND

First published 1975 by A & C Black Ltd.
4, 5 & 6 Soho Square, London W1V 6AD

© 1975 A & C Black Ltd.
ISBN 0 7136 1597 4

Also published in two parts (limp bound)
ISBN 0 7136 1454 4
ISBN 0 7136 1455 2

Filmset and printed in Great Britain
by BAS Printers Limited, Wallop,
Hampshire

Contents

Macmillan's Bicycle 1839 – the first to look at all like the modern version.

Preface

My initial aim in writing this book has been to present a panoramic background of Scottish social history against which may be set more detailed reading of the kind indicated in the book lists.

A secondary aim derives from the fact that in a book of this size it is not possible to include more than a small proportion of the total amount of historical material available; what I have chosen as relevant necessarily reflects my own interests and experience. I would hope therefore that *Life in Scotland* will stimulate readers to investigate places, persons, ideas and events other than those I have selected — to look at Jarlshof, perhaps, rather than Skara Brae and to encounter figures equally characteristic of the early eighteenth century as Captain Burt: people such as Archibald Grant of Monymusk, Andrew Cochrane of Glasgow or Allan Ramsay of Edinburgh.

In the interests of unity, I have blended material from different literary sources into one continuous narrative. The illustrations, though linked to the text, provide in some measure an independent and episodic narrative of their own. Some, such as David Allan's cartoons and certain of Slezer's drawings, are familiar — others have not been previously published. With few exceptions, I have drawn upon Scottish sources for the photographs and reconstruction drawings.

Norman Nichol

Drumlanrig Castle, a seventeenth-century country house, was built for William Douglas, 1st Duke of Queensberry. (He occupied it for only one day, horrified at the enormous cost.)

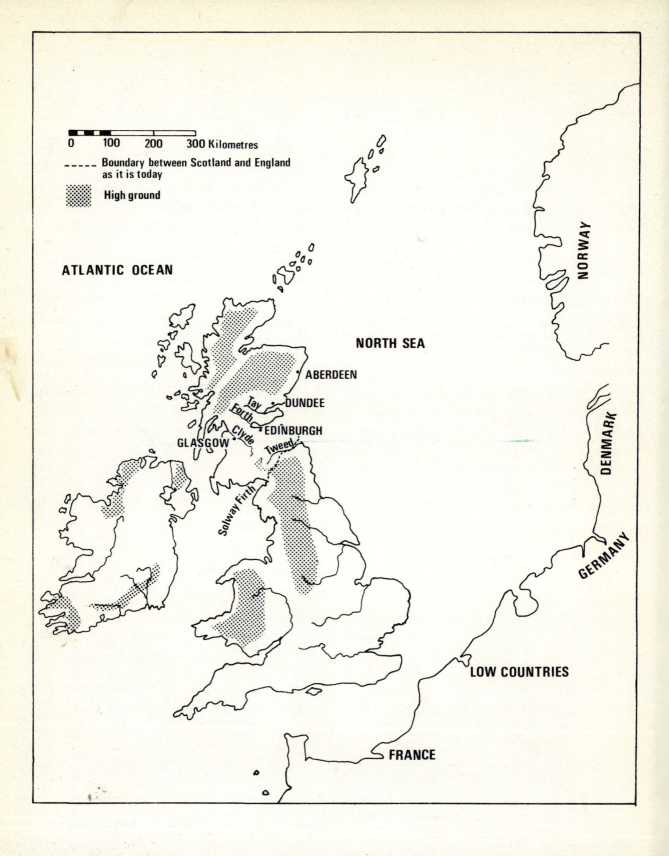

ATLANTIC OCEAN

NORTH SEA

NORWAY

DENMARK

GERMANY

LOW COUNTRIES

FRANCE

ABERDEEN

DUNDEE

Tay

Forth

EDINBURGH

Clyde

GLASGOW

Tweed

Solway Firth

0   100   200   300 Kilometres

- - - - - Boundary between Scotland and England
as it is today

High ground

Western Scottish coastal scenery has changed little since the strand-loopers first sailed to Oban and Oronsay. They would still recognise this modern view of Islay whose many caves and sandy beaches attracted later prehistoric settlers. Standing stones, cairns and burial kists are found all over Argyll and the neighbouring islands.

1 EARLY TIMES

Scotland was one of the last places in Europe to be settled because until about 8000 B.C. northern Britain was covered in ice. When the ice melted the sea level rose and the flat plain which had linked Britain to the rest of Europe was flooded, cutting off the flow of men and animals from the Continent.

Hunting tribes had lived in southern Britain for thousands of years but their numbers were small and they had no need to seek hunting grounds in the north. In any case marshes and forests made inland travel impossible, so that Scotland's early visitors all came by boat.

The first visitors, the *strand-loopers*, came to northern Britain about 5000 B.C., paddling up the wide firths of the west coast and beaching their skin-covered canoes on the sandy shores. They looked for dry ground clear of trees and undergrowth and for caves which they could use as homes.

The *strand-loopers* were summer visitors only. They spent their time fishing and then moved away westward to Ireland when autumn came. Hundreds of years passed before real settlers arrived, *Middle Stone Age* hunters who crossed the North Sea from Germany and Denmark or sailed to the south and west coasts from France and Spain.

Flint can be chipped to razor-edge sharpness. These finely shaped arrow heads of the New Stone Age were tied or gummed into the split ends of the arrow shafts.

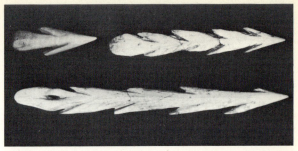

Early fishermen had no metal for fish hooks. These bone fish spears from Oban are barbed to stop speared fish from wriggling away.

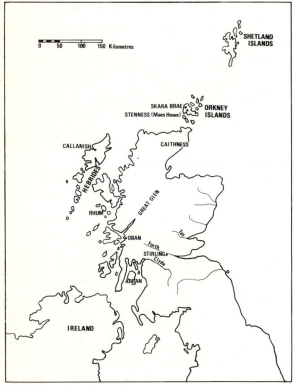

Maps in this book are designed to show where particular events and constructions took place and where particular people lived. The physical features of Scotland can be more clearly seen on the general map facing page 1.

The newcomers lived in family groups, camping beside the wide firths. In those days the Forth, the Tay and the Clyde spread over the flat lands which are now dry ground. The rivers and marshes yielded a good supply of food: fish, waterfowl and even sea-birds such as gulls and cormorants.

The men used bone weapons and fish spears for their fishing and they hunted with spears and arrows tipped with sharp flint. They made nets and snares and fish traps from plant fibres and they used heavy stone axes for felling trees and hollowing out logs for canoes.

Sometimes they used their axes on bigger game. In A.D. 1877 a whale's skeleton was found eight kilometres from the river near Stirling. It had a reindeer horn axe still in its skull, just as the hunters had caught it stranded in the shallows thousands of years ago.

The wandering hunters needed good hard stone weapons and tools. Flint was scarce and had to be brought from a distance. Other useful stones were discovered, bloodstone in Rhum and pitchstone on Arran. The supply of such

MIDDLE STONE AGE: The first settlers

stones was the first kind of trade.

About 4000 B.C. other peoples came to settle in Britain. These newcomers were different. They still hunted and fished but they were also farmers. When they landed they brought boatloads of young animals – cows, sheep and pigs – and earthenware jars filled with barley and wheat seed.

They, too, were people of the Stone Age but because they fashioned new sorts of tools and used the old ones differently they are known as *New Stone Age* people.

The New Stone Age farmers set up their homes on the west coast, in the Hebrides, the Great Glen, Caithness, Shetland and Orkney. Wherever they could, they settled near natural meadows and grassy plains where they could graze their cattle and long-legged sheep.

When they needed more farmland they used their stone axes to fell the old forests of oak, elm and ash, and slashed and burned down the undergrowth. The thick wood ash helped to fertilise the ground for their seed. They put the animals out to graze on the rest of the clearings.

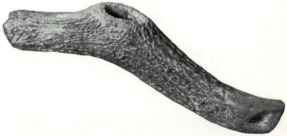

This reindeer horn axe from Stirling has been drilled to take a wooden handle. The wide flat horn made flensing knives to strip blubber from the whale's carcass. New Stone Age farmers used reindeer horn for spades.

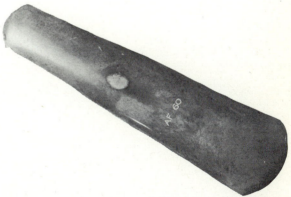

This stone axe head needed a long handle to make it effective. It could be wedged into a forked branch or a hole bored in a stout timber. Alternatively, the head could be lashed between two splints of wood.

NEW STONE AGE: The first farmers

Midhowe Cairn on Rousay Island, Orkney, is a huge mound of stone, 32 m long and 13 m wide. The long burial chamber inside, 23 m long and 2 m wide, has an inner wall of stones laid horizontally and an outer skin of slabs set herringbone fashion. Bones of sheep, oxen and birds show that burial feasts were held at the entrance. The chamber is divided into twenty-four stalls, twelve on each side. The bones of twenty-six people found in the chamber (17 adults, 6 teenagers and 2 children) show that the Midhowe people were short (about 1·6 m) and slender, with long narrow heads and faces. They were probably Mediterranean people, with black hair, black eyes and swarthy skins. Flattened leg bones suggest that they did not use chairs or stools but squatted on their heels. The bones also show that the adults suffered from rheumatism.

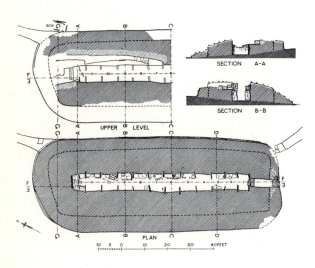

　　　　　　　　　　　　　　　　　　NEW STONE AGE: The first farmers

New Stone Age people found that clay hardens in the heat of a cooking fire. The maker of this pot decorated the wet clay before it was fired. The pot was preserved in a Chambered Cairn, part of the furnishing put there to please the spirits of the dead.

The saddle quern was one of the earliest pieces of kitchen equipment: grain laid on the flat stone was crushed by the rubber. The invention of the rotary quern, where grain is ground by the circular motion of the upper stone, made grinding much easier. See pages 27, 103 and 107.

The pattern of their lives was very different from that of the hunters and food-gatherers, because the needs of crops and animals laid down a daily routine for every season. For most of our ancestors it was a pattern that changed little until the coming of the steam engine at the end of the eighteenth century A.D.

The New Stone Age farmers certainly lived pleasanter lives than the hunters. The mixed diet of grain and meat was better for their health and they lived longer. What is more, there was a place for both old and young in the farming community for all could help in some way in the work of the farm.

There is little trace now of these early farmers and their lives, for soft materials like wood and leather and cloth perish quickly, but from Skara Brae on Orkney (see pages 6–8) we have learned a great deal about how similar people lived later, between 2500 and 2000 B.C.

We do know, however, that the New Stone Age people had strong religious feelings. When people died they were laid to rest in great tombs or burial cairns. Over a thousand of these have been found in Scotland.

Each burial place consists of one or more chambers where the bodies were placed, covered by a huge cairn of stones. Some are enormous, built of enough stone to build four or five parish churches. They seem to have been used again and again, the earlier skeletons pushed to one side to make room for the latest burial. Possibly people believed that the spirit lingered in the body until it withered away to mere bones.

There are many shapes and sizes of burial mounds but most Scottish cairns have a passageway or gallery inside, divided into chambers by big slabs of rock. At one end there is usually a fore-court which was used for religious ceremonies. Traces of fires and pits dug in the ground in special patterns tell us that the cairn was probably the centre for feasts, rituals and dances to please the gods, who might then make the herds increase and the land more fruitful.

Skara Brae people crawled along this passage-way to reach their homes, sunk deep in the refuse piled up to keep out the shrieking winds.

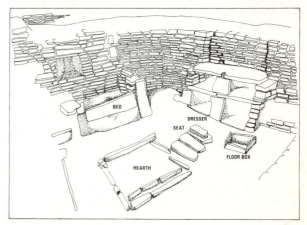

A typical house interior: the local flagstone splits neatly into flat slabs, which made the dry-walling and furniture-building easier.

The hunting and farming peoples mingled and intermarried in the centuries which followed, so that knowledge of farming and stock-raising spread through the country. One interesting late New Stone Age settlement was at Skara Brae, on the mainland of Orkney. It dates from about 2500 B.C.

The settlement was preserved for us when a great storm on the Bay of Skaill blew tons of sand on to the farmers' homes. The villagers fled before they were trapped and the village remained buried for nearly 4000 years until another storm blew the sand away again in A.D. 1866.

We know that Skara Brae was rather different from most farm settlements in northern Britain, because there was little wood on the island and both the houses and the furnishings were made of stone. Because of the fierce Orkney winds the people built their houses in a tight cluster, piling up their refuse outside until the village was almost buried and the houses could be reached only by a paved alleyway.

The seven houses that remain give a clear picture of a New Stone Age farmer's dwelling. The stone houses almost certainly followed the pattern of timber

This is a skeleton view of Skara Brae as it appears today, with the rubbish mound stripped away to show the houses and passageways. Note the paved courtyard in the foreground. The nearest house had been used as a kind of workshop by a stone worker.

houses found in wooded areas on the Scottish mainland, rectangular in shape, with rounded corners and a tent-like roof covering.

The stone walls at Skara Brae were thick, with a core of rubble held between well laid stone courses. Recesses were left as wall-cupboards and a dresser of stone was neatly built into one wall. The wall of one house was lined with blue clay and some of the houses had window holes.

The walls sloped in gradually from a height of a metre or so towards the ceiling and the gap was covered by whalebone or driftwood rafters carrying a turf roof.

The village had sewers and drains running under the stone-flagged floors out to the sea. In many ways the Skara Brae houses were better than some Orkney cottages used until the early nineteenth century, cottages which had the same sort of wall-cupboards and stone bed recesses.

People entered the one-roomed house by creeping through a low door cut in the thick wall. The door itself was a slab of stone (the local flagstone splits easily into layers), and could be held shut by a whale-bone drawbar whose ends slotted into notches cut in the wall.

These scrapers were used to clean the inside of the animal skins that were then sewed into clothes. Other pieces of flint and bone were used to bore holes to take the 'thread', probably animal sinews.

Skara Brae people used animal vertebrae and stone pots as paint jars, to hold the yellow and red ochres with which they painted their faces and bodies for special occasions.

The 'beads' from this necklace were found scattered on the floor. Perhaps the owner left hurriedly at the time of the storm and could not stop to pick them up. Animal teeth made easily matched 'jewels' for personal adornment.

Archaeologists cannot agree about the use of these carved stone balls, found only in Scotland. They may have been used as magic weapons or missiles, or they may represent the sun or moon and have religious meaning.

A peat fire smouldered in the centre of the floor, the bitter smoke finding its way out through a hole left in the roof.

Cooking was done at the flat hearthstone and the family used the stone bed frames as seats. Half-gnawed bones and the remains of a pot of beef stew show that meat was stewed or roasted; and piles of bones of young animals show that most of the cattle were killed off in the autumn. There was little to feed the beasts on in the winter.

Shell-fish helped out the diet. Each home had a little tank-shaped box of stone which may have been used to store the shell-fish. Red deer were hunted for venison.

The two big beds had skin canopies held up by stone pillars and the Skara Brae people slept snug and warm in their heather and skin bedding. Though they kept sheep the villagers do not seem to have known how to spin and weave, for there are no signs of the weights needed to stretch the loom threads. There are plenty of scrapers and borers, however, so we can imagine that the women spent a great deal of time scraping skins and sewing them into clothes.

New settlers arrived about 2000 B.C., the Beaker People from Holland and the Battle Axe People from Germany. Their fanciful names come from objects found in their graves. Many people were now buried separately in kists made of stone slabs, on their sides as if they were asleep. It is possible that the new arrivals believed that the dead would reawake in an after-life.

They were taller than the earlier settlers, averaging about 1·85 m, strongly built, with round-shaped heads. They inter-

Maes Howe, on the mainland of Orkney, is the finest New Stone Age tomb in northern Europe. The mound of stone is approximately 7 m high and 35 m in diameter. The burial chamber, a cube of about 5 metres, lies in the centre. It is reached by a passage 11 m long and about 1·2 m high, which is roofed with great rock slabs (megaliths) over 6 m long.

The burial chamber is of stone slabs so well smoothed and fitted that it is hard to slide a knife blade between them. The corbelled roof slopes inwards and is supported also by buttresses 3 m high. The dark recess is one of three burial cells set in the walls.

The Bronze Age brought many refinements in dress and ornament. Compare this arm ring from Crawford (Lanarkshire) with the Stone Age tooth necklace on page 8. Smiths could make any shape they pleased by pouring the molten metal into prepared moulds.

married with the earlier inhabitants and came to use the same sacred places as religious centres. Many of these places have been looked on as holy ground for thousands of years.

Near Maes Howe are the Standing Stones of Stenness and the Ring of Brodgar, put up by people who moved into the area after the Beaker People.

Three Scottish Beaker graves contained things new to the country, such as copper daggers from graves in Linlathen (Angus) and Glen Forsa (Mull) and a bronze arm ring from Crawford in Lanarkshire. These metal objects are a sign of the great change in tool-making which had been taking place on the Continent and in the Middle East.

BRONZE AGE: The beginning

This beautifully shaped bronze dagger, from Kilrie (Fife), would have been riveted to a decorated handle.

Prospectors now came to Britain seeking copper and tin for making bronze. Wealthy farmers and warriors eagerly sought the wares of merchants who traded in weapons, tools and ornaments made of bronze and gold. The smiths who worked in metal became important craftsmen.

Bronze sickles and axes made farm work easier. They enabled farmers to clear fields in the valley bottoms as well as on the hillsides. People no longer had to move away in search of food and lived in larger family groups which grew into large tribes.

There were religious changes, too. Very often people cremated their dead and put the ashes into funeral urns which were then placed in large enclosed cemeteries. The size of these cemeteries shows that generation after generation of Bronze Age farmers farmed the same pieces of land.

Swords like these were the treasured possessions of noble warriors. Hilt and blade were cast in one piece for strength and holes left for riveting a wooden handle to the hilt and blade.

Bronze Age warriors were fond of feasting and drinking. This cauldron would have been hung by chains over an open hearth and used for seething the great joints of pork and beef eaten at banquets.

The bronze smith's skill enabled him to beautify everyday objects of every kind. Hollow curving tips were fixed to cow horns used as wine cups, transforming them into elaborate drinking vessels.

The population grew steadily and tribes had to band together under war leaders to defend their own land or to seize their neighbours' farms. Successful war leaders became lords and kings, and built hilltop forts to defend their people against attack.

Bronze leaf-shaped swords, with sharp points and cutting edges, show that a class of warriors grew up in the seventh century B.C. They were skilled swordsmen, able to afford beautifully balanced swords designed for both slashing and stabbing.

Other metal goods of the same period include bronze cauldrons, horse harness and chariot fittings. They indicate that warrior chiefs were trading with the Celtic peoples of Europe.

The Celts were tribes of warlike and artistic people who settled in Europe about 850 B.C. and gradually spread westwards. They were horsemen and charioteers, great fighters, feasters and wine drinkers. Their craftsmen ornamented their metal work with skilful and fantastic designs.

In the fifth century B.C. many Celts crossed into southern Britain, conquering the inhabitants and setting up their own powerful kingdoms.

One reason for their success was their knowledge of iron working which enabled them to use iron swords and spears. Iron is a difficult metal to work because smelting the ore requires great heat; but the ore is more plentiful than tin and copper and makes a metal harder than bronze. Though iron tools and implements made the work of farmers and craftsmen easier, iron weapons made warfare more common and more deadly.

BRONZE AGE: The Celtic invasion

Reconstruction of the house at Green Knowe.

2 CELTS

New customs crept into northern Britain in the fifth century B.C. Some new settlers were refugees from the Celtic invaders further south, some were warrior bands in search of land. In the end a steady flow of iron-using Celtic peoples moved into the country.

Farmers began to build walls and palisades round their farmsteads to keep out marauders, more forts appeared on the hilltops and a new type of house, called a wheelhouse, became popular.

One of the earliest house sites found in Scotland is at Green Knowe in Peeblesshire. Archaeologists have been able to work out just how it was built. It is one of a group of houses built on a platform scooped out of a sloping hillside.

The builders began by setting up two circular wattle screens made of interwoven branches plastered with clay. They enclosed the floor space of the house, a circle 8·7 metres in diameter. The screens were placed about 85 cm apart, separated by a low wall of stones and the space be-

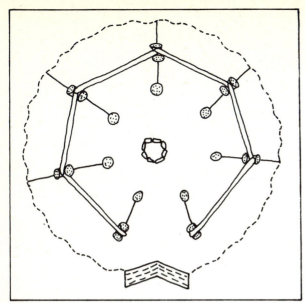

This diagram shows the plan of a wheelhouse: the circles of upright posts, the crossbeams, the partitions and the central hearth. The outer circle of posts carried the main weight of the roof, as stone walls did in the north. The gabled porch was roofed separately.

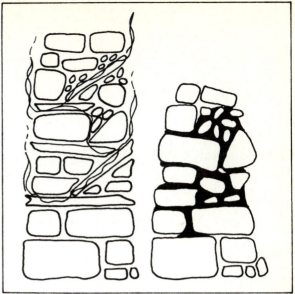

A drawing to give some idea how walls became vitrified. Where walls were built of stone and timber which caught fire, the heat of the burning timber melted the stone. The blocks of stone joined together as they cooled after the fire.

tween the screens was packed with grass and heather to make a warm insulated wall.

Eleven upright posts carried the roof timbers and a conical roof covered with skins or thatch, and the entrance was through a gabled porch.

Other houses of the period follow the same circular plan. In later houses there was no cavity-filled wall and the roof was supported on an outer ring of upright poles linked by crosspieces. Sometimes the eaves of the roof were extended to reach the ground, giving extra storage space.

This new pattern of house gave its inhabitants a spacious central room, and they arranged partitions like the spokes of a wheel to give private apartments and store rooms. In the north where there was little timber the people built wheel houses of stone.

The forts on the hilltops became stronger, defended by great ramparts of stone six metres thick. The fort-builders often laced baulks of timber among the stones so that they could not easily be battered down. Where the timber caught fire and fused the walls into a solid mass, they have been nicknamed *vitrified forts*.

The reason for building stronger forts was that the Celtic invaders brought war chariots and war horses as well as iron weapons.

IRON AGE: Houses and forts

This model of a Celtic chariot is in the National Museum of Wales. The craftsmanship of the original fighting machine is seen in the spoked, iron-rimmed wheels, the wickerwork sides, the curved hand-grips for driver and warrior (who both stood at the back) and the double yoke for the two ponies.

This statuette of one of the wandering professional Celtic warriors is in the Staatsmuseum of East Berlin. The naked warrior wears a belt, a helmet and the golden neck torque which was the warrior's chief ornament. (See also page 32.)

The chariots were light two-wheeled vehicles with wicker-work sides, built to carry two men, the warrior and his companion, the charioteer. The charioteer took no part in the actual fighting. His task was to drive his two small specially bred horses at full gallop into the enemy ranks.

As the chariot hurtled forward the warrior worked himself into a battle fury – then leapt down, sword in hand, to find a worthy opponent. His aim was to slice off as many heads as possible, while the charioteer withdrew to await his noble companion, who returned swinging severed heads in both his hands as battle trophies.

Their enemies must have found the Celtic battle charge a horrifying and impressive sight. Celtic warriors made an appalling din in battle. They rightly believed that sheer noise would unnerve

A decorative panel from the Gundestrop Cauldron, in the National Museum of Denmark, shows Celtic warriors in battle order, some on foot with swords, spears and long bossed shields, others on horseback. One can almost hear the warlike scream from the trumpets on the right. Their mouths are in the form of animal heads as in the photograph below.

their opponents. Battle began with the hoarse scream of the long curved war horns, and the warriors' battle cries added to the thunder of the horses' hooves, the earth-shaking rumble of the iron-shod chariot wheels and the clatter of horse and chariot fittings.

Warriors were proud of their magnificent appearance and most of them went into battle in their finest and most colourful clothes. They wore flowing cloaks, knee-length tunics and long trousers, all dyed in rich colours, purple or red, or woven in chequered patterns. Others fought naked except for their golden torque, or neck ornament. This was specially true of the bands of fighting men who toured the country selling their services to the leaders who needed extra warriors.

Their chief weapons were spears with huge iron blades as long as a man's fore-

This bronze trumpet mouth from Deskford (Banff) reflects the Celts' esteem for the wild boar.

arm and a span wide. They also carried long iron swords sheathed in decorated scabbards hung at their right sides, and leather shields, painted and decorated also. The elaborate designs on scabbard and shield were supposed to give magical protection in battle.

Sometimes they wore leather helmets, but more often they showed off their long flowing hair, bleached and stiffened with lime so that it stuck out from their heads.

These Celtic invaders spread their way of living throughout the country, conquering people already settled or intermarrying with noble families.

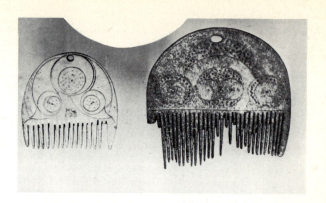

Mirrors like this polished bronze mirror from Balmaclellan were used by Celtic men and women. During the Bronze Age metal razors first appeared, allowing men to shave their faces. Bronze and bone combs were delicately decorated with the patterns that appear on many Celtic possessions and that may have had magical meaning. The combs were probably used as much for adorning as for combing the hair.

This piece of checked woven woollen material from Falkirk is the earliest known 'tartan'. (The pattern has been worked out in the diagram.) This gives an idea of the appearance of Celtic tunics and cloaks.

Warriors certainly enjoyed fighting and feuding but they spent a great deal of their time hunting deer and wild boar. They thought the wild boar the noblest animal of all because of its strength, ferocity and the courage it showed when it turned on dogs and hunters. They went fowling, too, using slings to bring down the birds. They were also fond of sports, athletic contests and field games (like the Irish shinty) which were a good training for hunting and battle.

They also liked music, feasting and dressing up for social gatherings and religious ceremonies. Both men and women were proud of their long hair, worn loose or plaited. Women often piled their hair into elaborate styles and used ornamental combs to hold it in place.

Women made cosmetics by brewing up dyes from herbs and berries. They reddened their cheeks and darkened their eyebrows, peering into polished metal hand mirrors. They also painted their fingernails.

They dressed in long tunics, gaudily coloured and striped or checked, which reached to the ground and, like the men, they had long woollen cloaks for outdoor wear. Often both tunics and cloaks were fitted with hoods.

Though they were fond of fine clothes and ornaments, their circular houses were very plain and poor. The Celts had been a race of nomads and wanderers, used to tents and rough shelters. Even when they settled down they lived in the open air as much as possible and cared little for furnishings and comfort.

Feasts were lively affairs, attended by both women and men. They sat on the rush-covered floor and ate from dishes set out on small tables arranged in a circle. They used their fingers to pick up chunks of pork and beef which were their favourite dishes. The meat was roasted on spits or seethed in cauldrons hung by chains over the open fire.

They drank heavily of home-brewed ale or wine and sometimes the banquets ended in brawls as warriors fought for the 'hero's portion', the thigh bone.

They were not gluttons, however, and they looked down on people who overate and who became fat and lazy. Though they enjoyed physical pleasures to the full, they had a great respect for things of the mind. Minstrels and story-tellers were eagerly listened to, and priests and law-givers were regarded as very important people.

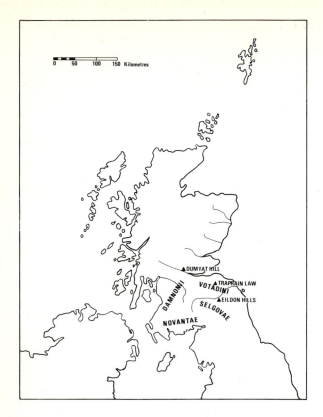

Celtic craftsmen were skilled at metalwork but less so in stone. This carved figure from Blackness Castle shows a Fertility God. Early farmers believed that such a god had power to bring good harvests and to increase livestock.

Their religion was mixed up with a deep belief in magic. Kings and priests had to know how to conduct sacrifices and ceremonies exactly, to please the gods. It took a priest twenty years to learn the magic lore from his master. Nothing could be written down and all the laws, rules and customs had to be learnt by heart.

Each tribe had its own special father-god and mother-earth-goddess. If they became displeased, the tribe would be defeated in battle and crops would not grow.

The Celts believed that their gods and goddesses lived in lonely places, in groves of oak trees, on hilltops, beside wells and streams and near burial grounds. They also had special shrines, such as Medionemeton (probably on Cairnpapple Hill, Lanarkshire), where feasting, dancing, games and sacrifices took place.

When warriors collected the heads of their enemies they did so for a magical purpose. The heads were stuck on poles at the gateways of forts and villages so that the spirits of the slain men would keep away evil.

We still celebrate some of the old Celtic feast days. Our Hallowe'en marks the end of the old Celtic Year and the feast of Beltane celebrated the time when ewes

The Selgovae had their oppidum on the north peak of the Eildon Hills (the one on the left of the picture). The Romans called the Eildon Hills Trimontium (there are three peaks altogether) and took over the oppidum as a beacon signal station.

began to give milk.

By the time the Romans invaded northern Britain in A.D. 78, the land was divided into great tribal territories. The Romans reported that the tribes south of the Forth–Clyde line were made up of three classes of people: kings, nobles and freemen. The noble class included lords, warriors and priests, lawgivers and prophets; the freemen included farmers who owned their own land and skilled craftsmen such as smiths. Below these there was a mass of people who had no say in tribal affairs; landless labourers, slaves and bondsmen.

Each tribe had its own hill-fort which was a tribal centre and stronghold. The Romans called such places towns (Latin: oppidum). The Selgovae had their oppidum on the northern peak of the Eildon Hills, near Melrose, the Votadini had a large settlement on Traprain Law, near Haddington, and the Damnonii had a fort at Dumyat Hill, near Stirling.

The forts and weapons of Iron Age times perhaps give the impression that North Britain was one great battleground. There were still very few people in the land; most of them lived out their quiet lives working their farms and herding their beasts, paying rents and taxes to king and lords in return for protection and peace.

This broch on Mousa, Shetland, still stands. The thick walls hold many staircases and galleries, and protect a small courtyard.

This model of a crannog (in the Kelvingrove Museum) includes a dugout canoe, needed to reach the island. Another access would have been along a winding causeway just below the surface of the lake, hidden from hostile eyes.

This drawing is of the Iron Age dun at Kildonan Bay, Argyll: a wall 5 m thick is pierced by a tunnel-like gateway and contains a gallery and a double staircase leading to the top. Timber houses would have filled the courtyard.

3 ROMANS

The Romans began to conquer Britain in A.D. 43 and bands of refugees and defeated warriors drifted northwards as the Romans advanced. The peoples of North Britain built new sorts of strongholds to protect their farms and territories, walled forts or duns in the west, and brochs in the east.

The brochs were most unusual in appearance, tall windowless towers over twelve metres high. The walls were made of two skins of stone with a hollow space between filled with galleries and stairs. They enclosed a circular courtyard about thirty feet in diameter, just big enough for a few families to shelter during a raid. Most of the brochs were set by the sea-shore so we can guess that the most dangerous enemies were sea raiders in search of slaves and booty.

During a raid the people inside were quite safe, even against fiery arrows and sling shots, for the only entrance was through a long tunnel cut through the thick wall.

People living in a low-lying marshy country built crannogs, little artificial islands near lakesides and river banks. The houses on the crannogs were protected by the water and by high palisades.

A Roman sandal from Trimontium. It was laced by a thong through the loops and round the leg.

These defences were not strong enough to stop a Roman army. When the Roman general, Agricola, came to North Britain in A.D. 78, some tribes like the Votadini decided to make friends with him. Others like the Novantae of Galloway fought back and the Romans ringed their territories with forts.

Within six years Agricola had tamed the land south of the Forth and Clyde. The main Roman garrison was at Newstead, in Tweeddale, near the old fortress of the Selgovae. The Romans built a beacon on top of the hill and used it as a signal station. They built harbours at Inveresk and Irvine so that ships could bring in grain to feed the army, and roads to link the harbours and the forts.

Then Agricola decided to tackle the tribes further north and built a new fortress at Inchtuthil, north of Perth. In A.D. 84 he took his legionaries and a strong force of cavalry into battle. They met the red-haired Caledonii and their allies at Mons Graupius (near Elgin) and soon put the painted and tattooed tribesmen to flight. Noisy chariot charges did not upset the highly trained and disciplined Roman soldiers. Agricola could do little more because the Emperor Domitian needed troops on the Danube and decided to withdraw some of the Roman army from Britain.

A Roman kettle from Trimontium, the headquarters camp near Newstead (Roxburghshire).

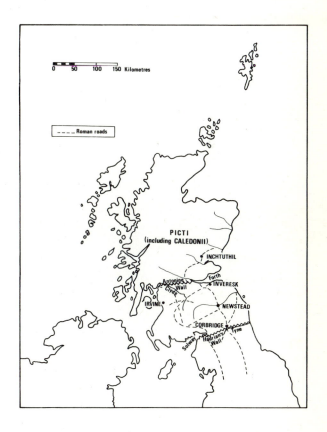

A carved stone from Bridgeness (East end of the Antonine Wall near Bo'ness) records completion of 4612 paces of the wall by the Second Legion. On this panel a Roman cavalryman rides down a group of naked Celtic warriors. Compare the shields with those on page 15.

An aerial view of Dere Street, the important Roman road, near Jedburgh. It was to be 1600 years before good roads were again laid.

This visor from Trimontium (for parade, not fighting) shows a Roman soldier's face.

Some of the Roman silver buried at Traprain Law, probably looted from the Continent.

Three legionaries from a tomb in the fort at Croy Hill, on the Antonine Wall. The Wall was a military outpost and had no civilian towns like those on Hadrian's Wall.

The triumphant legionaries had to dismantle the new fort at Inchtuthil and retreat south. They stripped the fort of timber and building materials and, disgusted at their luck, they smashed their spare crockery and threw it into the drains.

All that they had achieved in North Britain was to teach the tribes to band together under one war-leader. At Mons Graupius the leader was Calgacus, 'the swordsman', the only North Briton of that time whose name we know.

In A.D. 117 North British chariots raided down to the Roman base of Corstopitum (Corbridge) in Northumberland. Emperor Hadrian had a great stone wall built between Tyne and Solway in A.D. 125. He aimed to make this his frontier, but when the tribes kept up their raids the Romans decided to conquer North Britain again.

Hadrian's Wall followed the line of an inland cliff. It was carefully built to keep out raiders, with a milecastle every thousand paces, sentry walks and signal stations at intervals along the whole length and a cavalry fort every few miles. The best-known and biggest fort is Vercovicium (Housesteads). The wall snakes away over the crags beyond the fort. A small civilian town grew up behind the fort, which was guarded by a crenellated wall and four large gate towers.

Once more they took over the lands of the Novantae, Selgovae, Votadini and Damnonii. This time they built a wall of turf and timber across the narrow neck of land between Forth and Clyde. The wall, with its nineteen forts, was meant to keep out the tribes beyond, whom the Romans now called the Picts (Picti = painted men), but raids by land and sea still went on.

The Antonine Wall was the north-west frontier of the Roman Empire for about fifty years. Then the Romans fell back to the old frontier of Hadrian's Wall because they did not have enough troops to conquer the Picts and they gained little profit from this distant province. They kept some control over the lands south of the old Antonine Wall by sending out long-range cavalry patrols, until Hadrian's Wall was itself over-run at the end of the fourth century A.D.

There is little left of the Roman occupation apart from relics left by soldiers at forts and garrisons, because the Romans built no towns or villas as they did in the south of Britain. The biggest settlement of Roman times was the hilltop fortress of the Votadini at Traprain Law. It consisted of three hundred round Iron Age houses with inhabitants who were skilled craftsmen in enamel and metal. Coins and pottery from Gaul show that the Votadini had trading links with the Continent and certainly Roman roads and bridges made inland trade easy until the Middle Ages. Dress fastenings and brooches suggest that the Votadini never wore Roman-style tunics and togas but kept their own style of costume.

Whatever else the Romans left was swept away in the great raids carried out by the Picts and the sea raiders from Germany, Denmark and Ireland.

4 SCOTS

This picture of a Scot, drawn by one of the Irish monks who illustrated the illuminated manuscript known as the Book of Kells, shows him armed with spear and circular bossed shield and wearing tunic and breeches.

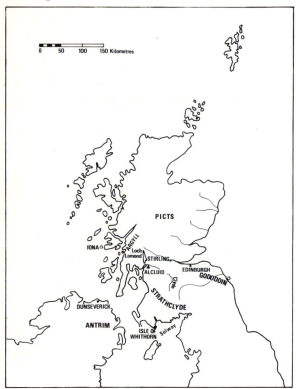

At the time that the Romans left there were many tribes in North Britain.

The Gododdin, the people whom the Romans had called the Votadini, ruled in the south-east. Their chief strongholds were on the great volcanic crags at Edinburgh and Stirling. In the fourth century A.D. a prince of the Gododdin, Cunedda, went to settle in North Wales. Much information about Britain at this time comes from Welsh poets who wrote in the common Celtic tongue.

The south-western tribes had joined together to form the kingdom of Strathclyde, which stretched from Loch Lomond right to the kingdom of Rheged on the Solway. Their great fortress of Alcluid stood on the twin-peaked rock which guards the entrance to the Clyde near Dumbarton.

The Picts still controlled the north, but their powerful kingdoms were to be challenged by new invaders from Antrim, Ireland. Like the North Britons, these newcomers were of Celtic origin. They earned the nickname 'Scots' (raiders) from the ferocious slave raids they carried out on the west coast of Britain in the fourth century A.D.

So many Scots then settled in the west that about A.D. 500 their king, Fergus Mor, left his Irish capital of Dunseverick and set up the kingdom of Dalriada in Argyll.

Seventh-century Irish laws describe the way of life of a well-to-do farmer in Dalriada. And Welsh sources suggest that all the tribes lived in a similar way, in kingdoms ruled by the chiefs who were heads of the most important kin groups.

Wealth was reckoned by the numbers of cows and slaves a man owned. There were no coins and people used cattle and slaves to bargain with, a woman slave being valued at four cows.

Farm stock probably consisted of a score of cows and two bulls, half a dozen pigs, twenty sheep and six oxen for drawing the plough. Every year the farmer planted sixteen sacks of grain. There were beehives in the enclosure, for honey was the only sweetening food available.

The farmers of Dalriada were fishermen, too. Their boats were curraghs, large boats with a timber framework covered with pitch-smeared hides and seven rowing benches, each taking two men. In time of war each group of twenty farmsteads provided the king with two boats and their crews.

These are the ruins of the Norman church built to replace the tiny white stone church ('candida casa') put up by St. Ninian on the Isle of Whithorn when he began to convert the Strathclyde people to Christianity around A.D. 400.

Two sickles and an iron-pronged rake from Trimontium show the kind of equipment used by farmers during Roman times and for many centuries afterwards. Basic patterns are much the same today but the tools are no longer much used by farmers.

Farm equipment was plentiful, with iron knives, shears, an adze, a saw, an auger, axe, hatchet and bill-hook. The design of craftsmen's tools was copied from those brought into Britain by the Romans.

The dwelling-house, like other buildings, had clay and wattle walls and a thatched roof. A cauldron, hung from the roof beams, bubbled over a peat fire which was never allowed to go out. Smoke from the fire helped to cure flitches of bacon hanging from the rafters.

There was another cauldron for special occasions, a huge bronze pot which could seethe a whole pig, and a spit for roasting meat. Other household equipment included a vat for brewing ale, kneading troughs for making bread and cups made of wood and iron. Wooden buckets held milk and ale.

There was also a pitcher and a wooden trough for washing. Water was heated by dropping heated stones into the trough, a very quick and effective method.

It was more difficult to arrange proper lighting. Richer folk could make tallow candles by boiling down the fat of animals slaughtered for eating. Poorer people used rush lights, made from the dried pith of bulrushes.

Both the farmer and his wife owned several changes of clothing – tunics with square cloaks held in place by a silver brooch. The tunics were often embroidered and fringed, sometimes with gold or silver thread if the wearer could afford it.

Girls and women were never idle, for as well as the usual tasks of looking after children, cooking and baking, they had to make most of the things that are now bought in shops. They spun woollen and linen thread, dyed it with colours made by boiling up lichens and berries, wove it into cloth and sewed the cloth into clothes. Then there was the endless grinding of corn and churning of milk to make butter and cheese as well as helping with the tasks of the farm. The poor bondswomen must have had a wretched existence.

A beehive-shaped monk's cell on Inchmacolm in the Forth — like those on Iona, but of stone.

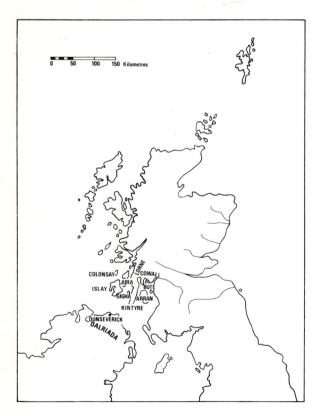

Loyalty to the kin, or family group, is found among all peoples. This feeling was very strong among the Scots living on the lonely shores and islands of Dalriada.

In seventh-century Dalriada the Scots were grouped into three peoples or tribes, each taking its name from one of the sons of Fergus Mor. The kin of Loarn lived in Lorne and Colonsay, the kin of Gabran took over Kintyre, Gigha, Jura, Cowall, Bute and Arran, and the smaller kin of Angus settled in Islay. The kin of Gabran became the most important. Descendants of their kings came in the end to rule over the whole of North Britain and to give 'Scotland' its modern name.

Though the Scots had learned men of noble rank who could recite the old laws and customs of the kin, they had no law courts where justice was done. If the laws

A drawing of St. Columba by Adamnan, the monk who wrote Columba's life story, in a manuscript now in Switzerland. It shows a slender long-faced priest, wearing a long-skirted, long-sleeved robe with a short wide-sleeved surplice on top – and hands raised in blessing.

The Monymusk Reliquary is a wooden case with bronze fittings, used to carry holy relics. Shaped like a house, with a sloping roof and a central roof beam decorated in the centre and above each gable, it gives a good idea of a seventh-century Celtic church.

showed a man had been wronged or injured it was up to his close relatives to seek revenge or to get damages in the form of money or cattle. The amount of damages depended on the wronged man's 'honour price', according to his wealth and importance.

The Scots of Dalriada brought with them from Antrim a new religion, Christianity.

Ireland had been Christian since the time of St. Patrick. The man who did most to bring Christianity to the rest of North Britain was the monk Columba who left Ireland in A.D. 563 with twelve followers and set up his own monastery on the island of Iona.

Columba was a fiery high-spirited nobleman, great-great-grandson of Niall, High King of Ireland, but he gave no thought to worldly comfort or luxuries. The monk who wrote his life story, Adamnan, says that Columba's study was furnished with manuscripts, chair and desk for study but his sleeping chamber had no furniture at all. Columba slept on the floor with a stone for his pillow.

His monastery on Iona was built after the Irish fashion, with a rectangular stone church and clay-and-wattle huts, bee-hive shaped, for the brethren. The buildings also included a refectory, kitchen and guest house.

Columba and his disciples spent a great deal of time outside the monastery, however, preaching, baptising and making converts all over North Britain. They taught a new idea of what was important in life and turned men's minds away from fighting and feasting and fine clothing.

One story tells how Columba chased a robber down to the seashore and cursed the evildoer as he fled – Columba standing knee-deep in the waves, his hands raised to heaven.

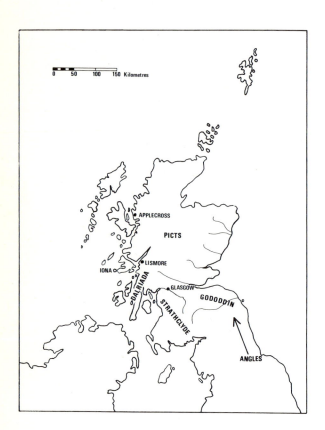

Columba himself set the pattern for later missionaries. Thin and worn by travel and fasting, he was always busy – reading, praying, working with his hands, consoling unhappy people and rebuking the wicked.

The sixth century saw a great deal of missionary work. Famous Celtic missionaries included St. Moluoc, St. Maelrubha who founded monasteries at Lismore and Applecross and St. Mungo who started a religious centre in Glasgow.

Mungo was friend and adviser of Rhyderch Hael (Roderick the Generous), king of Strathclyde, and Columba was friend and counsellor of King Aidan of Dalriada.

Celtic monasteries were looked upon as part of the whole community and their abbots reverenced as leaders of the people. In time of war the monks joined in cursing the enemy for they thought of their monastery as part of the kins who made up the kingdom.

The people of Dalriada spoke of themselves as 'Gaels'. Their language, Gaelic,

The seals of the Bishops of Glasgow all showed St. Mungo, his dress according to the date. Left: this may tell how Mungo, when jealous Roderick of Strathclyde threatened to kill his Queen for losing a ring, told a monk to catch a salmon – and the ring was in its mouth.

was a Celtic tongue not very different from the Celtic speech of the earlier North Britons.

The coming of Christianity also helped to bring a feeling of fellowship among the peoples living in North Britain. They had been converted and baptised by the same missionaries, they shared the same beliefs about what was right and wrong on earth and had the same hopes of the world to come. Their learned men could pass on news and ideas because they read and wrote the same language, Latin. Each monastery recruited a quota of clever boys who would themselves become Christian teachers, missionaries and churchmen.

Angle and Saxon 'sea-wolves' from Denmark and Germany conquered southern Britain in the fifth century A.D. When the Angles of Northumbria pushed gradually up the east coast of Britain to attack the kingdom of the Gododdin, they seemed all the more terrifying because they spoke a strange alien tongue, followed different customs and, above all, were heathens.

The Papil Stone, from the island of Burra, chief monastic centre of South Shetland, shows a Celtic Cross and, beneath, four monks carrying pastoral crooks.

DARK AGES: Celtic unity

5 ANGLES

The Gododdin were the first North Britons to face attack by the Angles. Sometimes they counter-attacked. The Welsh poet, Aneurin, records one of the many forays against the Angles in an old poem, 'The Ride of the Gododdin'.

He tells how 300 young warriors feasted and drank before they set out on their desperate raid. Being Christians, they also went to pray to God before setting out 'on swift horses with long manes', with gold torques about their necks.

Their journey took them 200 km south to Catterick, Yorkshire, and all were slain. Aneurin describes the warriors' appear-ance and the death of the last of this gallant company:

> *A light broad shield on the crupper*
> *of a swift horse,*
> *Clean blue swords,*
> *Fringes of fine gold.*
> *Before his wedding feast*
> *His blood streamed to the ground.*
> *Before we could bury him*
> *He was food for the ravens.*

The ravens and corbies had their fill of slaughtered warriors before the Angles succeeded in pushing their kingdom up to the Forth. They made Edinburgh their

headquarters. It is named after King Edwin of Northumbria.

The Angles who invaded North Britain were hungry for land and they fought so fiercely that for a time it looked as if they would conquer the whole country. Most fought with spears, throwing-axes and daggers, while nobles had swords, sometimes made from bars of iron that had been twisted together and then hammered into a flat blade. This gave the sword a marbled appearance.

All warriors carried round wooden shields with an iron boss covering the hand grip. Even if the shield splintered the boss made a very effective 'knuckle duster'.

The Angles dressed differently from the Britons. Men wore woollen tunics and linen trousers held tightly to the leg by cross-garters. These were strips of cloth fastened to their leather shoes and twisted round calves and thighs. Women wore long tunics of wool or linen, with the sleeves caught in at the wrist by small clasps, and a girdle whose ends were decorated with key-shaped ornaments. Often they carried a workbox hanging from the girdle, containing needles, thread and tweezers.

The Angles farmed their lands in North Britain in the same way as they had done in their own homeland. The most usual settlement was a *tun*, a village of small oblong houses protected by a palisade. Outside were large open fields where each farmer had his own strips of land. As the Angles were great believers in equality, the strips were scattered so as to give each man a share of the good and the poorer soil. They grazed their beasts on the common pasture.

A rich man had his own palisaded tun, with outhouses and perhaps a *bower* for the women and children as well as his great hall. This was a solid timber building with two rows of roof pillars supporting a gabled roof, which was often decorated on the outside by a set of spreading stag horns.

A bench for visitors was set outside and there was a place for them to leave their spears before going inside, where seats were arranged by the open hearth that ran down the centre of the hall. On feast days the lord sat in his High Seat halfway down the hall, his wife by his side and his guests of honour opposite.

The Angles brought new ideas which helped to shape the future of North Britain. Although Gaelic became the language of the north and west, the English (Angle-ish) tongue became the speech of the lowlands.

Like the Scots of Dalriada the Angles had kings, nobles and freemen, half-free bondsmen and slaves. They also depended on the kin to carry out the law and the family of an injured man had the right to take *wergild* (compensation) from the wrongdoer's family. Northumbrian laws laid down in very matter-of-fact terms just how much wergild was due for different ranks; a king 30 000 thrymsa, a noble 2000, a freeman 266.

Nobles and freemen attended a meeting where a man's guilt was settled. Each party to the quarrel had to produce twelve men who would swear an oath that their man was innocent. In small villages this was usually quite a good method, for everyone knew the rights and wrongs of the case. Sometimes the matter was settled by ordeal of fire or water; a known evildoer might be outlawed and, like a wolf, be killed on sight.

This is the first page of St. Matthew's Gospel, written and illuminated by the monks of Lindisfarne. Northumbrian monks excelled at producing beautiful manuscripts, decorated with scroll-work designs.

This eighth-century Cross, 5½ m high, is now preserved inside Ruthwell Parish Church, Dumfries. It bears an inscription in Runic characters (an early form of writing) which is the oldest example of 'written' English (Northumbrian dialect). Pictures and carvings told Bible stories when few people could read or write.

The Angles were converted to Christianity by two groups of missionaries, one from Rome and one from Iona. In A.D. 635 the monk Aidan went down from Iona to set up a great monastery at Lindisfarne. Other monasteries soon appeared, at Melrose, Abercorn, Jarrow and Monkwearmouth. Further south were other famous religious settlements at Whitby and Ripon, in Yorkshire.

In 663 King Oswy of Northumbria decided that Church affairs should follow the Roman pattern, with bishops and not abbots in charge.

This new organisation slowly spread to other parts of North Britain. During the seventh and eighth centuries the Northumbrian Church became the most active and brilliant in North Britain, with its famous saints – Cuthbert, who was born a shepherd boy in Tweeddale, Wilfred and Bede, whose writings became famous throughout Europe. A great deal of our present knowledge comes from Bede's *Ecclesiastical History*.

6 PICTS

The Pictish kings welcomed the Northumbrian missionaries, but they objected when the Angles invaded their territory. In A.D. 685 the Picts ended Northumbrian hopes of conquering the north by defeating the Angles at Nechtansmere.

The Picts left no written records to tell about their way of life, though it is known that they had a well-organised kingdom. The Pictish kingdom was by far the strongest and the least troubled by invaders until the Viking raids of the eighth century.

The carved monuments and pillars show that Pictish craftsmen were highly skilled. Early sculptors carved the stone slabs with beautifully designed animal figures and Christian artists of the seventh century specialised in interlaced stone crosses, the rest of the slab being filled with animal and human figures.

In most countries princes succeed to their fathers' thrones, but in Pictland the crown was passed down through the female side of the family. When Kenneth MacAlpin of Dalriada married a Pictish princess in A.D. 843 he was able to join the two kingdoms together to form the kingdom of Alba. From that time, the Alban kings made their headquarters at Scone.

A Pictish double-link silver chain 45 cm long, linked by a clasp engraved with Pictish symbols picked out in red enamel.

The Stone of Scone, coronation stone of Scottish kings, was the centre of many tales even before it was brought from Ireland, probably in the ninth century. Edward I of England thought it so important that he carried it off in 1297 when he tried to make himself overlord of Scotland. It still gives 'magic' power to the Coronation Chair at Westminster Abbey, London.

Picts often erected slabs of stone carved with a great Cross on one side, symbols and people on the other. This reverse side of the Cross-slab of Aberlemno (Angus) shows Pictish symbols (interlocked animal heads, a rectangle with a Z-rod, triple discs) and three rows of footmen and horsemen.

Viking silver coins from Birka in Sweden show long ships with striped or latticed sails, made from wood or leather.

A thistle brooch and other silver jewellery, part of a hoard of Viking loot found buried at Skaill, on the mainland of Orkney.

7 VIKINGS

Priests all over the British Isles began to read a special prayer in the eighth century A.D. as the Vikings began to plunder the coasts of Britain.

'A furore Normannorum libera nos, Domine!' they chanted. (From the fury of the Norsemen deliver us, O Lord!)

The Vikings (sea-raiders) sailed over from Scandinavia in long clinker-built ships propelled by oars or by a single square sail and built strongholds on coastal promontories. Then they seized horses and raided the countryside in search of slaves and booty.

After a while they began to settle in Eastern England and so weakened the Anglian kingdom of Northumbria that the kings of Alba were able to push their borders down beyond the Tweed.

Viking pirates from Norway captured the Orkneys in the eighth century and used them as a base for raids on the mainland. Some time before A.D. 900 the king of Norway himself, Harald Fairhair, took over the islands and appointed Earl Rognvald to rule them.

The Earls of Orkney ruled as if they were kings themselves, paying no heed to the orders of the King of Norway or the rights of their own freemen. The Norwegian custom was for all freemen to meet once a year at a *Thing*, or parliament, but

The ninth-century Oseberg ship was excavated in 1904 in Norway. Note the high carved prow, stern and bulwarks, and the clinker-built sheathing of the planks. The hull shape was designed like a work of art and ribs and strakes fitted afterwards. They were not nailed but lashed, to give elasticity to the hull in heavy seas.

their Earls had their own followings of noble warriors and did as they liked.

We know a great deal about the lives of the Earls and nobles from the great *Orkneyinga Saga* which describes the feuds, battles and sea-fights of heroic warriors. They were a bloodthirsty crew, with interesting nicknames such as 'Skull-splitter'. It is possible to visit the ruins of the *skaills* (great halls) today and see the exact places where they finished off their enemies. One usual method was to surround the enemy's dwelling at night and set it on fire (after allowing women and children to depart). The warriors inside had then the choice of burning to death or being pole-axed as they came out.

They had a very business-like attitude to raiding. The Viking Sweyn Asleifson (a leading character in the *Saga*) saw the seed sown on his farms before going off on a spring raid. Returning home laden with booty he watched his thralls gather in the harvest and then vanished on his winter foray.

Thorfinn saving his wife from the burning house.

Warriors lived in great style because of their booty. Sweyn Asleifson's hall at Langskaill measured 18 metres by 5 metres. The ordinary freemen were not so well off, even though they held their farms *freehold*, i.e. the land did not belong to an overlord.

Each farm stretched from hilltop right down to the low-water mark so each farmer owned all the foreshore as well. When a farmer died, however, his land was split among his children, sons receiving a whole share and daughters a half share. In the end the Orkneys were split into tiny farms too small to yield a decent living.

Vikings also captured the western isles right down to the Isle of Man and the Kings of Norway claimed the right to rule these lands until 1266. For years to come, the Viking customs and Norwegian tongue made the Orkneys, Shetlands and Hebrides different from the rest of the Scottish kingdom.

One of the greatest Orkney Earls was Thorfinn the Mighty, whose mother was the daughter of an Alban king. Thorfinn's army and fleet were strong enough to stop King Duncan recapturing Caithness and Sutherland in the eleventh century. When Duncan became king in 1043 he ruled the whole of modern Scotland except for the extreme north and west.

8 NORMANS

Other Vikings seized Northern France and, known as Normans, became the leading warriors of Europe. In 1066 Duke William of Normandy conquered the whole of England and six years later he brought a great army to Scotland when he came to complain about Scottish raids into England. Malcolm III (Canmore), now recognised as King of Scotland, agreed to accept him as overlord.

Malcolm III had no soldiers to match William's knights. They were as invincible as tanks, mounted on great war horses, clad in mail hauberks, with conical helmets fitted with nasals to guard their faces from sword slashes. Malcolm also thought that with William as overlord he would be able to call on Norman help if his enemies inside Scotland tried to overthrow him.

When Malcolm's son David I became king in 1124 he determined to copy Norman ways. David had married an English heiress, Ada de Varenne, who brought him estates in Huntingdonshire and Northamptonshire. As Earl of Northampton, David saw how the Anglo-Norman king, Henry I, kept a tight grip over England, using his nobles to help him govern the country.

The monks of Abernethy built this tall round church tower in the tenth century as a place of refuge during the disturbed times that followed the Viking raids. The influence of Celtic architecture was still strong in Abernethy, once the capital of Pictish kings. Inside, the tower has numerous floors of timber; it served the monks as belfry, treasury and place of refuge. The tower has probably been rebuilt at some time, because the lower courses are of grey freestone and the rest of the building is of yellow.

Mail-clad Norman knights with kite-shaped shields and long spears, from the Bayeux tapestry – embroidered in France to record the story of how the Normans overcame the English army.

David I and his grandson, Malcolm IV, from the Kelso Abbey Charter. Both are dressed in full regalia, with long robes, crowns, swords of state and ankle boots with pointed toes. The illuminator has interwoven a Celtic design of animal heads to form the initial M.

Each great noble was granted land by the king and in return agreed to serve him in battle, in his council chamber and in his law court. The noble also promised to send mounted knights to serve the king for forty days when the king had need of soldiers.

The nobles then doled out part of their land to their own followers, in return for the same promises. Below these lesser nobles were knights owning just enough land to pay for their equipment and horses. At the bottom of the 'pyramid' were the mass of ordinary people – freemen and serfs who tilled the land.

The amount of land needed to keep an armed knight was called a *fee* or *feu*, and this way of sharing out the land is known as the Feudal System. Even today, we find traces of the system in Scotland. Many householders pay feu-duties to a Ground Superior who now owns land that once belonged to a feudal overlord.

The first Norman nobles that David brought into Scotland came from his earldom of Northampton. Among the earliest to arrive was Robert de Brus, given land in Annandale, Ranulf de Sules who took over Liddesdale and Hugh de Morville who received Cunningham and

Duffus Castle, near Elgin, was first built of timber on the mound in the picture. Wood was later replaced by stone. (See also page 50.)

Lauderdale.

They took their surnames from the estates and villages they had owned in Normandy. Others, like the Stewarts, took their surnames from the new posts they took up under the Scottish kings. The first 'Stewart' was Walter FitzAlan, whom David made High Steward of the Royal Household.

By the end of David's reign in 1153 Normans held estates all over the lowlands, bearing names now common in Scotland: Agnew, Boswell, Barclay, Bisset, Beaton, Colville, Crichton, Cummin, Fraser, Gourlay, Grant, Hay, Lindsay, Maxwell, Montgomery, Sinclair and many others.

They brought many followers in their train whose surnames came from their occupations. The Fletchers were arrowmakers and the Lorimers were saddlers.

David also appointed sheriffs to look after law and order in the lands surrounding the royal castles and our modern shires are based on the old sheriff's lands. Over the sheriffs were justiciars who toured the country to make sure that sheriffs did their duty and that feudal lords kept law and order on their own estates.

Melrose Abbey, founded by Cistercian monks from Reivaulx Abbey (Yorkshire) in 1136, was destroyed in border warfare in 1545. Today, the red sandstone shell survives – pointed archways, flying buttresses and elaborate window tracery. The ruins inspired Sir Walter Scott to write (1805) 'The Lay of the Last Minstrel' which revived interest in medieval history.

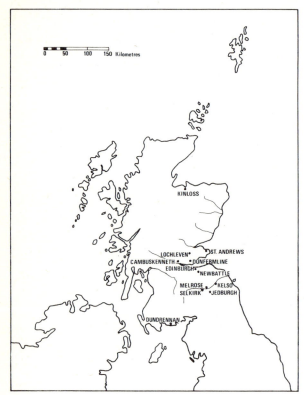

As the new lords arrived the lowlanders wondered at their clean-shaven faces, cropped hair and foreign tongue. The newcomer might be a great lord, with a small army of men-at-arms and a retinue of women and children, courtiers and servants. Sometimes it was a soldier come to take over a single knight's fee.

Often the new lords were abbots who had been granted land to support new monasteries. Augustinian monks settled at Jedburgh, Cambuskenneth, Holyrood, Lochleven and St. Andrews. New Benedictine abbeys appeared at Selkirk and Kelso to match the abbey at Dunfermline founded by David I's mother, the saintly Queen Margaret.

There were also Cistercian abbeys, set in the finest farmland, at Melrose, Newbattle, Dundrennan and Kinloss. The abbots did not think wooden buildings were good enough for Christian worship and foreign craftsmen came to build stone abbeys and churches.

The people went along with the land. The Abbot of Kelso's Charter mentions 'lands, meadows, men and pastures' all in one sentence. Feudal lords often looked on their *nativi* ('natives' or serfs) as no better than beasts.

Indeed, when John Vesey gave lands to Melrose Abbey his clerk described a native's family as a *sequella* (a following), the same word used to describe a litter of pups.

Feudal lords could buy and sell their serfs if they pleased. In the twelfth century Osulf the Red and his son Walter fetched ten merks and Turkil Hog and his sons and daughters as well as all their future unborn descendants were sold to the Prior of Coldingham for three merks (a merk was two-thirds of a pound).

Usually it was much more profitable to keep the serfs on the land for, amongst other things, they owed the lord three days' work each week. Red-headed Osulf and Turkil who looked after the pigs were valuable parts of the estate.

A serf had few rights. Even his wife and children were the lord's property and the serf paid a fine (tax) when his daughter married. If she married someone outside the village the serf had to ask the lord's permission and pay a *merchet* to make up for the loss of her labour and her future 'litter' of children. A serf's son might be a clever boy picked out by the priest to serve the church but, again, the father had to pay a fee before he could leave the land.

St. Margaret's Chapel, named after David I's mother, is all that remains of the original castle of Edinburgh. The thick stone walls leave room inside for only a tiny chapel. St. Margaret's Norman kind of Christian belief and worship were to overcome the Celtic in the end.

Left: an abbot in ecclesiastical robes. His crozier has the crook turned inwards to show that he rules inside a monastery. Right: a bishop, similar in rank, has a crozier with crook turned outwards to show that he rules over a wide diocese.

Lack of feeding stuff meant that few farm animals were kept alive in winter. For fresh meat, landowners kept pigeons in huge dovecotes. Peasants hated the birds for raiding crops.

9 Middle Ages: PEASANT LIFE

Not all the peasants were serfs but they all had to pay special taxes. When a peasant died, for example, the lord was entitled to take the best cow as a heriot before the son could take over his father's rigs of land. If the man had only three cows, the lord could take his best possession instead, a brass pot or a woollen cloak or some other article of value.

Part of the rent was in the form of service and each man had to do certain work for the lord. This included fetching and carrying according to the season of the year and the lord's bailiff carefully noted how many *carriages* (cartloads) of wood, peat, stone, slate, soil or manure were due from each peasant. Those who failed to do their duty could be fined in the lord's law court.

At harvest time the peasants took their corn to the lord's wind or water mill to have it ground, paying a fee to the lord and grudgingly giving a *fourpit* to the unpopular miller. They had to provide new millstones when the old ones wore out and re-thatch the mill roof when it rotted.

In return for these services and duties,

The watermill was one of the earliest power-driven machines. A hillside stream had some water led off over the mill wheel – the water then flowed back into the stream further downhill. The rotating wheel turned the grinding stones inside the mill. Prestonmill, near Haddington, is an excellent example, now preserved by the National Trust.

the peasant farmer was protected from his enemies by his lord and his rights were looked after in the lord's court just as the lord was protected and given justice in his overlord's court.

In addition he had the right to graze beasts on the common pasture and take a fair share of peat and kindling from the waste land. He was also entitled to rigs (strips) of farmland in the great open fields that surrounded the settlement or *farm toun*.

The best cultivated land, the Infield, was made up of the rigs close to the cottages and carried the main crop of oats, *bere* (barley) for making ale, a patch of flax for making linen and a few rows of peas.

The Outfield was never fertilised at all and the farmers grew patches of oats until that piece of soil was exhausted and then left it fallow till it recovered.

Men of the toun lived off the produce of their own rigs but they banded together for heavy tasks like ploughing, pooling their draught oxen till as many as a dozen beasts were yoked together.

Ploughing : the picture shows every detail of the wooden plough, harness and ox-yokes as the beasts drag the heavy instrument along the furrows.

Harvesting : men and women work together – the women cutting the ripe corn with sickles while the man binds and stooks the sheaves of cut stalks.

One man went ahead with his iron-tipped wooden spade to shovel away as many stones as he could and behind him came another, with the straw rope reins of the oxen twisted round a wooden cross-piece. He walked backwards, watching the ground, so that he could stop the oxen and lead the plough clear of stumps and boulders that could not be moved. A third man had to guide him along.

A fourth man, the strongest in the team, held the plough handles, ready to take the shock of the ploughshare driving against a stone or root. The whole team moved ponderously up the rig, leaving behind a long snaky furrow, while a boy trudged alongside to urge the oxen along. He carried an ox-goad, a six-yard pole with a sharp point.

Other tasks were equally heavy, whether it was swinging a hand sickle at harvest time, threshing the corn with a wooden flail or winnowing it by throwing it up in the air by a barn door or on a hilltop.

Wives and daughters tended the sheep and goats, which had to be milked as well as the cows. It was their job, too, to clean out the byre which filled one end of the

Flailing and winnowing: corn had to be flailed to separate the grain from the stalks and then winnowed to clear the grain of chaff. Farming methods changed little till the eighteenth century.

This woven woollen hood, with its enormously long fringes, was found preserved in a bog in Orkney. It was probably worn by a fourteenth-century woman.

Three-legged pots and kettles for cooking food and heating water could be set securely among the embers on a flat hearthstone.

cottage and to carry the manure to the dung-heap outside the door.

They looked for the eggs which made up the part of the rent that was paid in kind, along with the oatmeal, barley, sheep and pigs their menfolk provided. They spent hours churning milk into butter, with a few cow hairs thrown in to help the fat globules stick together and perhaps a frog put in the churn to speed things up. Then there was water to be drawn, wood to be collected, meal to be ground down in a hand quern and wool or linen to be spun into yarn for making clothes.

Housework took little time. There was no more furniture than in an Iron Age dwelling: a chest for meal or linen, a rack for wooden cups, plates and horn spoons and a three-legged milking stool. Peasants slept on heather or straw beds in wall recesses or on the floor, warm amid the reek from the peat fire and the drowsy cattle on the other side of the wattle partition.

Peasant life was hard, but it was not all work. The Church had many saints' days which brought breaks in the usual routine.

The Motte of Urr, near Dalbeattie, Kirkcudbright. This aerial view shows the earthworks (mound, bailey and ditches) of an Angle or early Norman fortification. Earthworks of this sort were the first stage in creating a castle.

The most popular pastimes were singing and dancing. Many of the dances were very ancient, handed down from prehistoric times and each toun had its expert dance leader who knew the right steps and actions. Some dances recalled heathen celebrations, seed-time and harvest-time, and in others the dancers acted out old plays and legends. Sometimes the dancers dressed up for the occasion, as children do today for Hallowe'en.

As they danced they sang, using old verses from the past and new ones made up to suit local happenings, and ending each verse with a well-known chorus. In some places the Church did not approve the dancing and singing and told the people of the wickedness of their merry-making and drinking.

Sports were popular, too: wrestling, swimming, feats of strength and skill, and football. This was a very rough and dangerous game. Some peasants spent so much time at football that James III in 1447 ordered that 'football, and golfe, be utterly cryed down and not to be used'.

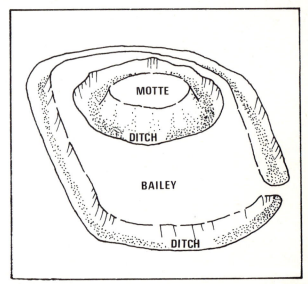

A diagram of the Motte of Urr, based on the aerial view above. The different parts of the earthworks are labelled. These were common to most castles in Norman times.

This reconstruction of Dirleton Castle, near North Berwick, shows a castle enclosed by high curtain walls and fortified with unassailable towers, machicolations and wooden fighting platforms.

10 Middle Ages: CASTLE LIFE

The new lords built castles for protection, usually on a hilltop. Early castles were built of wood. The first task was to dig a great encircling ditch, the soil being thrown into the middle to form a *motte*, a mound with a flattened top, up to sixteen metres high. A wooden palisade ran round the edge of the motte. Inside stood a wooden tower, protected by the palisade, the steep slope of the motte and the ditch below. The only way into the castle was by a bridge leading from the bailey (courtyard) which contained the barracks, stables and workshops. The bailey was itself protected by a palisade and ditch.

In the thirteenth century the feudal lords began to build in stone. The lesser gentry preferred a stone tower, with stables and storeroom on the ground floor, living room on the first floor and private rooms and attics above.

The great lords built castles which were enormously expensive. High curtain walls enclosed the castle courtyard, with battlements and sentry walks reached from the corner towers. The courtyard contained workshops, stables and quarters for servants and soldiers.

Caerlaverock Castle, near Dumfries, was built in the thirteenth century to guard the invasion route from the Solway. Most of the nearest tower and the lower part of the walls date from 1300; later additions have left the triangular plan of towers and curtain walls unchanged. The double gate towers and drawbridge gave extra strength to the entrance.

The main building was the donjon, a great tower with a hall and private rooms for the lord and his family. In the foundations was the pit, the dark funnel-shaped dungeon into which the lord could have prisoners lowered.

The weak part of the castle was the gate and so it was defended by a drawbridge spanning the ditch or moat, and an outer gate which in later days became a barbican, a small fort which had to be captured before attackers could tackle the drawbridge.

Behind the drawbridge was yet another gate, iron-studded, and a portcullis which could crash down at a second's notice. The tunnel between gate and portcullis was itself a trap and defenders could rain murderous missiles or boiling liquid through a hole in its roof.

The grim stone buildings were damp and draughty and the narrow windows admitted as much cold air as light. The lord and his family had to wear long fur-trimmed robes inside the castle, though tapestries, panelling and rushes took some of the chill from the stone floors and walls. Open fires and braziers were needed all year in the cold climate.

Life in the castle was more splendid but not much more comfortable than life in the peasant's cottage. There was not much furniture even in the main living room, the great hall, and the servants had to set up trestle tables before they could call the lord and his family to dinner.

The family and important guests took their places first. The lord had his own high-backed chair, but the rest made do with cushion-covered stools. The high board stood on a dais, with a great silver *salt-fatt* in the middle. The rest of the company sat on benches at tables placed down the centre of the hall, 'below the salt'.

Knives and spoons were set out on the high board, which was covered by a linen cloth. Other people had to provide their own. All had to use their fingers to eat with, for there were no forks, so eating was a messy business.

People often shared plates and cups. It was thought polite to offer friends choice pieces of food from one's plate and drinks from one's cup. Important people had

plates of silver, pewter or wood but lesser people ate their meat from large slices of bread (trenchers). The gravy-soaked slices were given to the poor.

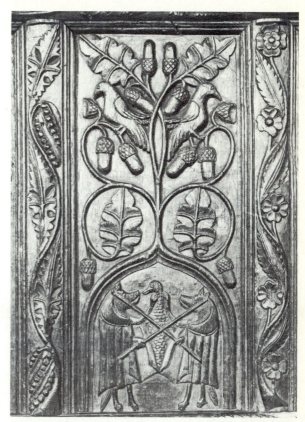

Oak panels like this one from Abbot Panter's hospital in Montrose reduced draughts. Friars are mockingly shown as foxes by the carver.

Valances were both decorative and draught-excluding. This detail shows allegorical scenes.

A lord and lady dine in great state, with minstrels to provide music and servants to carve meat and pour wine. The lady, in plain wimple and simple robes, is dressed less fancifully than the lady in ermine-trimmed gown on page 56. One dog licks a beggar's feet.

Food was plentiful (including spit-roasted joints of beef, pork and mutton, venison and fish), but it often came cold to the table as kitchens were on the floor below or in a separate building. Servants brought finger bowls and napkins so that the diners could rinse their fingers before the second course was served: sweet-meats made from nuts, preserved fruits, honey and herbs.

Dinner-time was enlivened by enter-tainments, provided by minstrels, lute-players, harpists and storytellers and the antics of the lord's jester.

At bed-time the lord and his lady retired to their bed chamber, simply furnished with feather bed and chests for clothes and valuables. They hung their long trailing robes on perches sticking out from the walls. Retainers, servants and visitors slept wherever they could find room, on the floor of the great hall, on benches, in corridors, or, often more comfortably, in stables, byres and kennels.

In bad weather the nobles amused themselves with chess, draughts and dice. Their usual pastimes were hunting and hawking, building up skills useful in war.

MIDDLE AGES: Life in a castle

Chessmen from Lewis, carved from walrus ivory about A.D. 1200. The costumes of kings and bishop are carved in fine detail. The warrior-pawns – with long shields, conical helmets and broad-bladed swords – have grim and terrifying expressions!

The nobles were warriors by profession. A boy's education began in childhood when he was sent to some great man's castle to train as page and squire. A great deal of his time was spent in learning how to handle weapons and how to control his horse in battle conditions. It was a rough and brutal training, but the boy also picked up some ideas about courtesy and chivalry which would help him to behave properly in high society.

He learned how a hero should behave from the long ballads sung by the minstrels whose songs filled the long evenings after supper. Tales of Arthur and Charlemagne and their knights became popular in the later Middle Ages and inspired many noblemen and their followers to ride off to join the Crusades. Those who returned brought more civilised ideas of behaviour and comfort, learnt from their Saracen enemies.

They learned from Churchmen, too, that a knight should do his best to defend the weak, see that justice was done, and defend the Christian faith. Some knights became members of chivalric orders which laid down the rules of knightly behaviour.

The first clarsach (sounding strings, from Gaelic) was probably brought to Scotland by Christian missionaries and became a popular musical instrument. This fifteenth-century clarsach (known as the Lamont Harp) from the House of Lude, Perthshire, is one of the oldest in Europe.

Medieval ladies spinning and weaving: of the three in front, the two on the right prepare wool for spinning and the one with the peaked headdress spins with a distaff under her arm and a spindle hanging from her right hand.

The quarrels and feuds of Scottish nobles, marked by murder, cruelty and treachery, show that many paid little attention to the Church's teaching.

The Feudal Age in Scotland lasted right through until the sixteenth century and it was very much a man's world.

Overlords had the right to marry off the orphan daughters and widows of their followers and they chose as husbands the men who would pay most. (When a woman married her property passed to her husband.) They married their own children to husbands and wives whose lands would increase their own wealth and power.

Yet women were as proud and high-spirited as the men. Black Agnes, Countess of Dunbar, defended the castle for six months when it was besieged in her husband's absence.

A nobleman's wife had great responsibilities in feeding and supplying the needs of the castle household. In many ways the castle was a kind of factory. Women pickled meat, preserved fruit, brewed ale, made candles, soap and dyes and stocked their homes with home-made blankets and sheets. There were no shops to turn to in time of need.

The thirteenth-century bridge over the Nith at Dumfries, built at the order of Devorgilla, youngest daughter of the Lord of Galloway. She married an Anglo-Norman lord, John Balliol, and when he died she built the Abbey of the Sweet Heart in memory of him. She had been well educated by her English grandfather and brought a civilising influence to Galloway's wild society.

MIDDLE AGES: Womenfolk in castles

The tower of Dalmeny church (west of Edinburgh) is new, but the rest of the church dates from Norman times as can be seen from the rounded arches over windows and doors.

11 Middle Ages: THE CHURCH

David I granted lands to bishops and abbots in just the same way as he gave land to his nobles. Many landowners copied his example and in the end about one-third of Scotland was ruled by Churchmen.

Newbattle was one of the great Cistercian monasteries, with estates all over Scotland. Its property included pasturage for a thousand sheep and sixty cattle given by Philip of Evermel, Lord of Lynton and Romanno, lead mines in the Lanarkshire hills and a quarry and a coal-mine on the sea cliff at Prestonpans. The abbots' serfs were mining coal there in the twelfth century.

The abbots ruled their lands like any other feudal lords, ready to put on their armour and join their high-born relatives on the battlefield. The great difference was that Churchmen were well educated and kept in close touch with other Churchmen in Europe. They studied the arts of farming, visited Church estates elsewhere, and their lands were better tilled and their flocks of sheep finer than those of the barons and the peasants. Newbattle wool was the finest in Scotland.

A reconstruction of the Cistercian Abbey at Melrose (see page 44). The abbey church is on the far side, with the enclosed cloisters and court-yard in front. The kitchen can be picked out by its great smoking chimney. The two large blocks to its left are first the Refectory, then the Dormitory with corbie-stepped gables. Between the Dormitory and the church are the Chapter House and the Parlour.

Fifteenth-century monks at one of the many daily services. The style of furnishings and dress has changed little over the centuries.

The different orders of monks followed different patterns of living. The Cistercians stayed inside their monastery walls, vowed to a life of prayer. They worshipped together at regular hours of the day and night. Clad in white robes, they spent some time working in orchard and garden but most of the heavy work was done by lay brothers, who did not take the full vows of the monks. The monks gave themselves completely to the work of God, promising never to marry, never to own any goods and never to disobey the orders of the abbot.

The Benedictine monks, the Black Monks, followed a similar life of prayer and work. The Augustinian monks, black-clad also, spent more time outside the monastery, especially on work connected

Glasgow Cathedral, first consecrated in 1136, dates mainly from the thirteenth century when it still contained relics of St. Mungo. Unlike most cathedrals it came unharmed through the Reformation.

with the great cathedrals.

A cathedral was the most important church in the diocese, the area of the country looked after by a bishop. One of David I's first acts was to appoint bishops to oversee the work of the Church. The largest and wealthiest diocese was that of Glasgow, which covered most of the old kingdom of Strathclyde, but the Bishop of St. Andrews was looked on as the most important Churchman of the country.

Bishops and abbots were men of noble birth, often younger sons who entered the Church because there was little chance of inheriting lands of their own. Well educated, used to running large estates, they served their kings as counsellors and chancellors and ambassadors.

To the ordinary people they were splendid figures, glimpsed as they rode along the highways with great retinues of Churchmen and men-at-arms. Peasants and craftsmen knew best the Parish Priest and the Friar.

The Priest was one of their own kind, a man of humble birth who during the week worked away on his piece of land as they did. His task was to hold Mass and perform the sacraments of baptism, marriage and burial.

The parish church itself was usually a simple stone building given by the lord of the estate to win favour with God. The lord also granted enough land to the church to pay the priest's stipend and therefore chose who the priest should be. The parishioners brought their own stools or stood during the service.

By copying manuscripts and writing letters, monks working in such a Scriptorium (writing room) kept learning alive in the centuries before the invention of the printing press.

It was not part of a priest's duty to preach sermons. Most of the preaching was done by wandering friars, Franciscans (Grey Friars), Dominicans (Black Friars) and Carmelites (White Friars). The friars owned nothing except their sandals and the rough woollen robe of

A friar preaches from a portable pulpit to an open-air congregation seated on the ground. Even in churches there were no seats until after the Reformation (pages 78–79). The friar is barefoot: he would own almost nothing.

their order and they depended on the charity of villagers and townsfolk. They gave up their lives to helping the sick and spreading the word of God among the people and did much to keep faith in Christ alive when other Churchmen became too rich and worldly to worry about helping the poor and needy.

Religion played a great part in peoples' lives. They knew that their earthly life was short, hard and uncomfortable, and looked forward to a heavenly life which would make up for the miseries they often suffered between birth and death. The Church brought the hope of better things to come.

The Church kept the country in touch with the wider world of Christendom. Each monastery had its scriptorium, where monks copied books written by philosophers, thinkers, scientists, poets and authors of the past. Cathedrals, abbeys and churches had their own schools for training monks and priests and sometimes they were open to other children, too.

Bishop Rae's bridge stood in Glasgow from 1340 to 1850. This view shows it when Thomas Telford had added footwalks on either side. The oak foundations were still solid after 500 years.

12 Middle Ages: BURGHS

David I and his successors saw how merchants and trading cities in Italy, France, Flanders and England paid taxes and customs duties to their rulers and made them wealthy. In the twelfth century Scottish kings set about creating merchant communities and trading towns of their own (called *burghs*) so that Scotland's raw materials – wool, skins, hides and valuable furs – could be exported in return for the luxury goods made by Continental craftsmen.

Some of the burghs were in new places, at the foot of royal castles. Others were set up at river mouths, fords and cross-roads. Most of them were tiny. The oldest and biggest burgh, Berwick (then in Scotland), numbered only 1500 inhabitants in the thirteenth century.

Kings attracted foreign merchants just as governments do today, by offering pieces of land rent-free for a year. They guaranteed special trading rights, royal protection from robbers and trouble-makers and freedom from paying taxes to feudal overlords. Their promises were written down in special charters, and each new burgess promised to pay a money rent to the king for his tenement and toft (house and land).

When Alexander II wished to gift a piece of land to Melrose Abbey, a charter was written out on parchment and made legal by being stamped with the king's private seal.

The sixteenth-century town port at St. Andrews: by the later Middle Ages most burghs had stone ports (gates, from French). Everyone had to leave and enter by the ports which were closed at nightfall and guarded by town officers in time of pest (plague, from French) and trouble.

McKeachnie's Close at Kirkcudbright follows the line of one of the medieval wynds that led off from the High Gait or main street to the houses and gardens of burgesses. As burghs had town walls right round them, burgesses were expected to seal the far end of their gardens by high fences.

The first burgesses came from England, Denmark, Normandy and especially from Flanders. There were so many *Flemings* that it became a well-known name in Scotland. They were strangers in a strange land, unpopular and unwelcome. They soon found it necessary to build a palisade round their wooden houses to protect their goods and lives.

Burghs had the right to hold regular markets and the peasants who came in to sell their products had to pay a toll to the gate-keeper who stood at one of the burgh *ports*.

There was usually one straggling main street, the High Gait, on to which the gables of the houses backed. Crooked *vennels* and *wynds* led off to the burgesses' houses, booths and gardens with their byres and malt barns. Burgesses eked out their living by cultivating strips of the town's farming land, brewed their own ale and kept a few cows which were looked after on the burgh common by the town-herd.

In the centre was the Market Cross, where stalls were set up on market day, and a Tolbooth, where merchants paid

Above : the tolbooth at Crail (Fife). From being a booth where merchants paid tolls, the tolbooth became the central government building of a burgh, housing council chamber, law court, offices and town jail. Below : carving of a tron, from a house at Ceres (Fife). The right to operate a tron and to collect tolls was an important burgh privilege.

The mercat cross at Aberdeen dates from 1686 when it replaced a medieval cross. The mercat cross was the centre of trade on market day and the most important burgesses set up their stalls closest to it. Stallholders were usually allowed stalls no more than an ell (1·14 m) wide. Goods bought and sold there would be weighed at the tron and taxed at the tolbooth.

customs duties after their bales of goods had been weighed at the Tron, the public weighing scales.

The burgesses paid no feudal dues and performed no feudal services. They kept law and order themselves and each resident took his turn with spear and lantern at night patrol (Watch and Ward). By day each burgess had to be ready to intervene and stop any brawling and quarrelling and burgh laws said he had to keep a steel bonnet, leather jack and long-handled weapon in his booth.

They settled burgh affairs at *Head*

Courts. Three times a year the burgesses streamed out to an open-air meeting place, often on a hilltop. Here, on the Moot Hill, they called the roll to make sure everyone heard old laws read out and new laws made. This was very necessary for few people could read and write.

Then they elected the bailies who would serve as magistrates for a year. They chose Town Serjeants who would carry out the bailies' orders, Tasters (to check the quality of wine and ale), and Apprisers (to inspect the quality and price of goods offered for sale).

They also watched while new burgesses were admitted. To be a burgess, a resident had to belong to the merchants' guild or a craft guild. Sons who inherited their father's property received a stone and a clod of earth as a sign they now owned the toft and a hasp and staple to show they had taken over the tenement.

It was difficult to become a guild member. First of all, a boy had to find a master who would accept him as an apprentice and then he spent years learning his trade. Apprentices were not entitled to any wages but their masters had to give them food and lodging, teach them and keep them under control.

After seven years, the apprentice craftsman had to pass a test by making his masterpiece which showed he had acquired perfect skill in his craft. If he were poor, he might then work as a *journeyman* and receive daily wages, hoping to save

enough to set up his own business. If he were wealthy, he could set up as a master craftsman himself. Burgh guilds did their best to keep out craftsmen from other places by making them pay large entrance fees.

To become a member of a merchant guild, a boy had to serve a five-year apprenticeship, learn the arts of commerce and go overseas with a cargo at least three times.

Guild members elected a Deacon to look after their affairs, and a Treasurer to keep the guild funds. Each member paid a contribution to the funds which were used to help sick members, widows and orphans.

Craftsmen in Scottish burghs made goods for the local market only. The only people allowed to trade abroad were the members of the Merchant Guild. They exported raw materials and imported manufactured goods that local craftsmen

could not produce – also spices and precious stones. As overseas trade flourished the merchants became much richer than the craftsmen and became the real rulers of the town.

As well as a weekly market, the burghs were allowed to hold annual fairs, which brought merchants and customers from all over Scotland. The countryfolk came in, too, to set up stalls and to gaze open-mouthed at the crowds of people and the entertainers who travelled from fair to fair. There were gaudily clad minstrels, acrobats, jugglers, dancers, story-tellers, mummers, men with dancing bears, peddlars selling ribbons and trinkets, wrestlers, fortune-tellers and vendors of charms to bring good luck.

There were also thieves and cut-purses (people had no pockets but carried their money in money-bags hung from their belts).

This marriage lintel above a house door in Falkland (Fife) records the marriage of NM to AO in 1610. In those days it was every apprentice's hope to marry the master's daughter – a certain passport to success.

MIDDLE AGES: The burgh fair

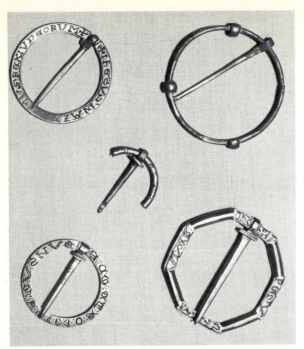

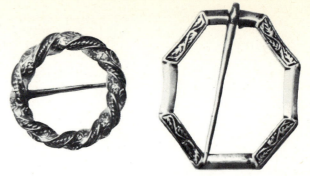

Medieval silver brooches were of a pattern still common today. But they were more than decorative: they pinned cloaks, for example.

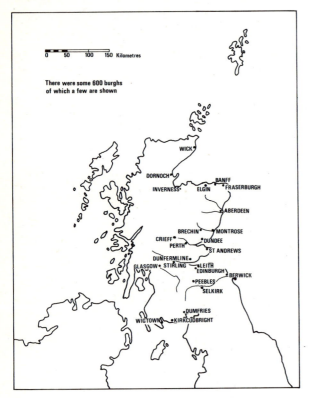

0   50   100   150 Kilometres

There were some 600 burghs of which a few are shown

WICK

DORNOCH

INVERNESS   ELGIN   BANFF   FRASERBURGH

ABERDEEN

BRECHIN   MONTROSE
CRIEFF   DUNDEE
PERTH   ST ANDREWS
DUNFERMLINE
GLASGOW   STIRLING   LEITH
EDINBURGH   BERWICK
PEEBLES
SELKIRK

DUMFRIES
WIGTOWN   KIRKCUDBRIGHT

Special law courts were set up to deal with petty crimes and disputes. They specialised in giving quick judgements, for the travelling merchants could not afford to wait for long drawn out arguments. The courts were known as Courts of Pie-powder (Norman French *Pieds pouldreaux*: 'dusty feet', possibly the nickname of travelling merchants) and they had to deliver their verdicts within 'three tides'.

The bailies held their own burgh law courts every two weeks, to deal with minor crimes. People were quick-tempered and quick to act, readily belabouring each other with whatever weapon came to hand – cudgel, stone, pot or dried fish. The usual punishments were a reprimand, a fine or a public apology.

Known criminals were punished more severely by flogging, branding, banishment or being nailed by the ear to the tron. Cases meriting death were kept for the sheriff's court.

As burghs became more important they had a kind of parliament of their own, the Court of the Four Burghs (originally Berwick, Edinburgh, Roxburgh and Stirling). The east coast burghs became the richest because they were closest to the Continent: Aberdeen, Edinburgh and Dundee, together with Perth, became the most important by the fourteenth century.

The Battle of Bannockburn, 24 June 1314, from the fifteenth-century manuscript by Fordun, the 'Scotichronicon'. Robert the Bruce's foot soldiers defeated a powerful English army of 20 000 men led by Edward II and won Scotland's freedom from English control. The artist shows the long spears used successfully against the heavily armoured English knights. Stirling castle and burgh are in the background.

13 Middle Ages: KINGS & NOBLES

The government set up by David I and his successors brought peace and prosperity to the lowlands. The orderly feudal system even spread into the north as more Norman lords were granted estates. The only part of the country where the kings had no control at all were the islands ruled by Norway.

Scotland's 'golden age' ended when Alexander III was thrown from his horse in 1286. There was savage warfare for the next fifty years as the great lords fought for the crown and the Scottish people struggled to keep Scotland free of English rule, first under Wallace and then under Bruce.

The wars brought enormous destruction. Edward I of England's army destroyed Berwick in 1296 and slaughtered its men, women and children. Border abbeys were looted and burned.

In 1328 the English finally had to recognise Scotland as an independent kingdom. The tragedy was that after Robert I (the Bruce) died there was no king strong enough to keep the great lords in check. Many landowners did as they pleased while sheriffs and justiciars could do nothing to control them.

Jedburgh Abbey, after centuries of border warfare, was finally ruined in the 'Rough Wooing'. (The English wanted Mary to wed Edward VI.)

James I (1394–1437) was a prisoner in England until 1424. On his return, he called a Parliament and passed an Act requiring a firm and sure peace throughout the realm – badly needed after 100 years of weak kings. James was murdered by unruly lords after thirteen years of good rule.

This picture of James II shows the king in the costume of the period. He is wearing hose, a short padded doublet, pointed shoes and a round low-crowned hat.

One of the most unruly subjects of King Robert III (1390–1406) was his own brother Alexander, Earl of Buchan. Nicknamed the 'Wolf of Badenoch' he plundered as he pleased and with his 'wild, wikkit hielandmen' burned down Elgin Cathedral.

In the highlands clan leaders and their clansmen were just as wild and uncontrollable. Men from Clan Chattan and Clan Kay settled one dispute, in the king's presence, by a thirty-a-side fight with swords, daggers and axes on an island in the Tay at Perth.

In the fifteenth century, however, kings tried to get control of their turbulent kingdom and to make all their subjects respect their authority. They all died violent deaths, James I and James III being murdered by disgruntled nobles after they had imprisoned and executed

A silver groat of James III's reign, about 1473. This coin, in which the silver is debased with cheap metal, is an early attempt at depicting a king's real features and the first coin with a thistle as a Scottish emblem.

some of the wilder lords and chiefs. James II and James IV died in battle.

In spite of their short reigns they helped the country's progress by calling Parliaments to help pass good laws, and by seeking the advice of educated counsellors instead of warrior lords.

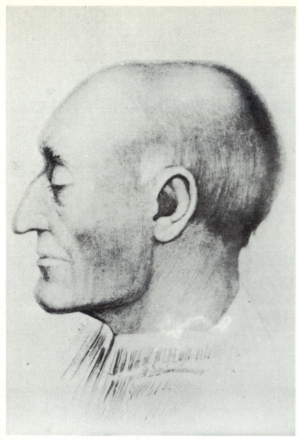

Bishop Kennedy, a reconstructed picture.

St. Salvator's College, St. Andrews.

14 FIFTEENTH CENTURY

One of the most famous king's counsellors was Bishop Kennedy of St. Andrews (1408–65) who encouraged trade and shipbuilding, farming and education. He built St. Salvator's College in St. Andrews, where the first Scottish University opened in 1411. Other bishops helped to found universities too. Bishop Turnbull at Glasgow (1451) and Bishop Elphinstone at Aberdeen (1495).

The opening of universities meant that Scots no longer had to go abroad for their higher education. It brought learned scholars into Scotland and encouraged nobles and burgesses to send their children to school as a preparation for a career in the Church, in government and law. The College of Surgeons, opened in Edinburgh in 1505, gave Scotland a head start over other countries in building up medical knowledge and skill.

Many burghs took a great interest in the local abbey or church school, providing money and land for buildings and paying the master's stipend. The Church had to approve the choice of schoolmaster, however, and kept on claiming this privilege right into the nineteenth century.

The *Auld Pedagogy*: old school buildings in Rotten Row, Glasgow, which were used for the first University of Glasgow. The University moved in 1561 to new buildings in the High Street.

James IV had Jacques Terrel build him the biggest battleship known. The 'Great Michael' was 72 m long and 11 m wide. Fore and main masts bore square sails, mizzen and bonaventure had lateen sails. The ship needed 300 sailors and over 1000 soldiers. Sold to the French after James' death, the ship that had taken all the oakwoods of Fife to build gradually rotted away unused.

Noble families converted their medieval castles into Renaissance mansions whenever they could. This house, with large windows and decorative stonework, was built in the courtyard of Caerlaverock Castle (see page 52).

The burgh schools were attended by older boys who had already learnt to read at home or in a *dame school*. Burgh schools were called grammar schools because the boys spent most of their time studying Latin, the language in which all learned books were written. They had to be able to speak the language as well as write it, for all university lectures were given in Latin and the different peoples of Europe found it a useful common language. Lawyers, doctors, Churchmen and royal officials had no difficulty in making themselves understood abroad.

The school day began early, at 7 a.m., and went on till evening, with breaks for breakfast and lunch. A lot of the work consisted of learning rules and passages by heart, but there was written work too.

James IV was in many ways a modern 'Renaissance' king, with a great interest in the arts and in science. In 1507 he granted a licence to Walter Chepman and Andrew Myllar to set up the first Scottish printing press. Their first production was the Aberdeen Breviary, a book of tales and ballads. They also printed poems by Robert Henryson, Gavin Douglas, Sir David Lindsay and William Dunbar, whom the king encouraged to write. In one book of poems, they included their 'arms', shown above. James IV still had a medieval desire to do battle and this led him into war with England. He perished at Flodden in 1513 – one of countless hundreds.

The boys, dressed in long tunics, carried leather satchels containing paper, ink horn, quill pens and a pen-knife for sharpening them.

Discipline was strict and boys were punished if they spoke in English instead of Latin. Very often one of the boys was set to spy on the others and report rule-breakers to the master.

There were holidays, however, and some schoolmasters were interested in sports and athletics. James Melville of Montrose was one of a small number of boys who went to a small boarding school and they spent a great deal of time learning to run, jump, swim, wrestle, handle the bow, fence and play golf.

James IV, who became king in 1488, was highly interested in education and in 1495 passed a law ordering nobles and wealthy burgesses to send their sons to school.

James was unusually well educated himself, well-grounded in Latin and able to speak French, German, Flemish, Italian, Spanish and Gaelic. He was energetic and active, highly interested in all sorts of activities, shipbuilding, gunnery, languages, science, music and literature. His great wish was to see Scotland as strong as France or England and he saw very clearly what its weaknesses were.

He encouraged trade and shipbuilding to build up the country's wealth, brought in skilled foreign craftsmen to help the Scots acquire new skills, and he successfully tamed (for the time being) two parts of the country which other Scottish kings had never been able to govern properly.

The claymore (big sword) was a two-handed sword wielded by the chosen warriors who were the chief's tacksmen. On state occasions it was a symbol or sign of authority.

The tombstone of Ranald, fourteenth-century Lord of the Isles, shows him armed with sword and lance and dressed in some kind of plaid.

The first area was the old kingdom of Dalriada. Since 1146 it had been governed by the descendants of a war leader named Somerled who styled himself 'Lord of the Isles'. In the fifteenth century the Lord of the Isles was the chief of the MacDonald clan.

The Lords of the Isles ruled just as Dalriadan kings Fergus and Aidan had done in bygone days. Their great painted galleys travelled the seaways, high-prowed and high-sterned, rowed by twenty-four oarsmen or driven by square sails of brightly coloured wool.

They toured their territories continually, collecting rents, settling disputes and meeting other clan chiefs in council. Here the chiefs sat at table, the walls of the room lined with men armed, highland-style, in tunics and coats of mail and planned how to deal with the king of Scotland and the king of England.

The Lords were crowned like kings, clad in white robes to show their purity of heart. At the coronation ceremony the Lord mounted a great square stone and set his feet in the footprints carved there. Then he was handed his wand of office and presented with a long handled clay-more.

The white wand of office was to show

The difference between high-lander and lowlander is shown by comparing these seventeenth-century pictures from John Speed's map of Scotland with those on page 80. The high-lander (often spoken of as Irish) kept to the traditional dress – a plaid of checked wool for the man and a plaid and long dress for the barefooted woman.

that he would rule fairly and honestly. The claymore was a sign that he would protect his people and their traditions.

Too often this meant a tradition of trouble making. In James IV's reign they feuded with the Mackenzies, seized Inverness castle and ravaged Cromarty. James IV was powerful enough to interfere. He brought the west under the control of royal sheriffs, pensioned off the Lord of the Isles (who came to live at the royal court) and made friends with the other highland chiefs.

In some ways the end of the rule of the Lord of the Isles meant that disorder was likely to increase. All through the fifteenth and sixteenth centuries the clan chiefs increased in power. Many clan leaders had Anglo-Norman names, Stewart, Fraser and Chisholm, and others were descended from Viking raiders.

Despite their Viking descent, their common language was Gaelic, and their way of life was like that of the Celtic peoples of Dalriada. The people living under a chief looked upon him as being the head of the kin and took his name as their own.

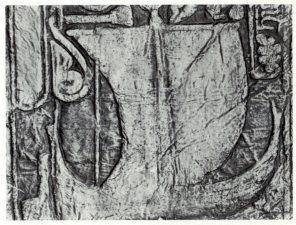

A west coast square-sailed galley carved on a grave slab on Oronsay, Argyll. A cast from the slab is in the National Museum of Antiquities.

An illustration from Scott's 'Lay of the Last Minstrel' shows moss troopers driving off cattle – small undersized beasts by modern standards.

The second troublesome area was the borderland between England and Scotland. Borderers took part in every war in the Middle Ages, led by the Douglases in Scotland and the Percies in England. Even in times of peace, they raided their English or Scottish neighbours from autumn to spring, driving off herds of cattle and horses.

In spring and summer they grew oats, barley and rye on their farms and grazed their cattle and sheep in the hills. In the autumn they got ready for the raiding season, before horses and cattle were weakened by lack of food.

Great cattle raids were planned like battles but small raids depended on knowledge of the countryside. Moonlight nights were good for raiding and it was safest to wait until just after the king's judges had made their annual tour.

Ordinary borderers lived in small stone-built thatched houses as other farmers did. Richer borderers built block-houses of thick oak beams and covered the roof and walls with turf so they could not be

Smailholm Tower, a peel tower near Kelso, was set in wild and rugged countryside. The door was fortified and living rooms on the upper floor could be reached only by a turnpike stair, set clockwise so that an attacker could not use his sword easily.

A detailed and lifelike study of a border reiver in the famous statue at Galashiels. He wears a steel bonnet, leather jack and high riding boots and carries a long spear as well as a sword. Horses were not usually as big as this one until a later period.

set on fire.

Great men had peel towers, three or four storeys high, defended by a stone wall. The only way of capturing a peel tower was to smoke the defenders out or get on the roof and break in from above.

James IV settled the Borders as he settled the other outlying and disorderly parts of Scotland. He rode in person with the justices and saw that severe sentences were carried out. His 'Jedburgh Justice' was famous long afterwards, but it did not cure the reivers, a rough, hard lot.

Steel bonneted, with leather coats covered with plates of metal and horn, with high boots and spurs, the reivers scoured the border country on their light fast horses till the reign of James VI. James IV died at Flodden in 1513 and three years later the borderers returned to their wild ways. When the Humes met the king's officer, the Warden of the Marches, in 1516, they killed him, cut off his head and took it home in triumph, tied by the hair to a saddle bow.

Lamb's House, a block of burgesses' houses in Leith, restored by the National Trust.

15 SIXTEENTH CENTURY

During the reigns of James IV and James V many burgesses grew rich as overseas trade grew. The chief foreign trading town was Veere, in the Netherlands, where the ruler gave special protection to Scots merchants and their goods.

From the Continent came a steady supply of luxury goods the Scots could not manufacture themselves – damask, velvet, fine linen and woollen cloth, arms and armour, gold and silver plate, looking glasses, parchment and books, as well as spices, wine, vinegar, medicines and perfume.

Burgesses replaced their wooden houses with solid stone buildings. Usually the ground floor was taken up by a booth and the living rooms reached by an outside forestair. The rooms inside were often low and small but in the hall (living room) the rafters were hidden by brightly painted ceiling boards.

Furniture was still expensive, mostly imported from Flanders but a wealthy burgess could now afford a real bedstead with four posts, a canopy and curtains. Merchants and their wives dressed in the height of fashion, breaking the laws which said they should wear sober, quiet clothes.

Bearded and dignified merchants from a carving on the Merchants' House, Glasgow. Such merchants benefited greatly from supplying luxury goods to wealthy Churchmen.

Many Churchmen lived in much greater splendour. Adam Colquhoun lived during the reigns of James IV and James V in one of the cathedral manses of Glasgow. It was a tall narrow house, with wooden balconies overlooking the gardens and orchards sloping down to the river Molendinar.

His rooms were crammed with carved Flemish furniture, settles, chairs, tables and chests. At night Adam slept in a carved four-poster bed, protected from draughts by damask bed curtains embroidered with silk and gold.

His wardrobe chests were full of fine clothes, velvet doublets and waistcoats, Holland linen shirts, hose from Paris and fur-trimmed mantles.

Adam drew salaries for four different church posts. It is not surprising that he

James V and his first wife Madeleine. She was the daughter of François I of France and the panel of her dress shows the royal French emblem, the fleur-de-lis. James holds the Lion of Scotland. Madeleine was too delicate to survive the cold wet Scottish climate and died two months after the wedding, at the age of sixteen. For his second wife, James V chose another French princess, Mary of Guise. Their daughter was Mary, illfated Queen of Scots.

had forty pieces of silver plate in his cupboards and a strong box full of jewelry and money.

What does surprise us is that one of his favourite pastimes was coursing hares with greyhounds, and that he owned not only an archery set, but a complete suit of armour as well.

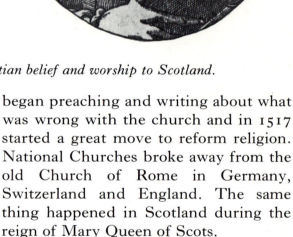

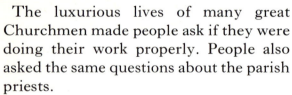
The reformer George Wishart was burned as a heretic on the orders of Cardinal Beaton. Wishart's friends then murdered the Cardinal in revenge. They were eventually condemned to be galley slaves. Among them was John Knox, at one time Wishart's bodyguard. After being freed, John Knox became a follower of John Calvin, a Frenchman, and brought the Calvinist kind of Christian belief and worship to Scotland.

The luxurious lives of many great Churchmen made people ask if they were doing their work properly. People also asked the same questions about the parish priests.

Very often the money set aside to pay the parish priest went to a wealthy abbey instead and ignorant ill-paid *vicars* were put in charge of the parishes. Some did not know the meaning of the Latin prayers they gabbled and some could not even read. Parishioners objected to paying tithes to the church when they got nothing in return and they complained bitterly when priests took a share of a dead man's property.

The invention of printing helped reformers to put these criticisms into easily read books. In Germany Martin Luther began preaching and writing about what was wrong with the church and in 1517 started a great move to reform religion. National Churches broke away from the old Church of Rome in Germany, Switzerland and England. The same thing happened in Scotland during the reign of Mary Queen of Scots.

Mary had gone to France as a little girl while her mother, the French princess Mary of Guise, ruled as Regent in Scotland. She called in French troops to put down the reformers, who were led by the fiery preacher, John Knox.

The reformers asked Elizabeth I of England to help them, and she sent up an army and a fleet. They besieged Mary of Guise's soldiers in Leith and when she died in 1560 the French hastily left. When

Mary Stuart in white, the colour worn as mourning dress after the death of her father-in-law, Henri II of France. She became Queen of Scotland and France for one year, from 1559 to 1560 when her husband, François II, also died. Then, at the age of nineteen, she returned to Scotland, a foreigner in her own country.

This portrait of James VI as a child shows him wearing a flat cap and long-sleeved doublet, with starched and ruffled collar and cuffs.

Queen Mary came back to Scotland in 1560 she found that a new Church of Scotland had been set up. Her reign was an unhappy one and in 1568, after a civil war, she fled to England and her baby son, James VI, became king.

There were dreadful civil wars during his childhood and these made James VI determined to make Scotland peaceful when he grew up. He succeeded, partly because he was well educated, clever and crafty, and partly because he inherited the throne of England when Elizabeth I died in 1603.

This carved rocking cradle, from Traquair House in Peebleshire, is said to have been used by the baby James VI.

Whereas the highlanders, shown on page 73, kept to the traditional dress, the 'Scotch' (Speed means here the lowlanders) had changed their costume over the centuries to match general European fashions.

16 UNION OF THE CROWNS

After 1603 kings very rarely visited Scotland. Instead, they ruled it through Parliament and a civil service of lawyers and administrators. As James said, he could govern Scotland by the pen. The kings of Scotland, for the first time, had enough wealth and power to see that their orders were obeyed.

He left behind him a country peaceful as it had never been before. Compared to England and France, Scotland was still a small and poor country, with a total population of under a million.

Most of its people still lived by farming and its growing burghs were still small. Edinburgh, Dundee, Aberdeen, Perth, Glasgow and St. Andrews were the biggest and most of the others numbered only a few hundred burgesses.

Scotland's future lay in trade, commerce and industry. At the close of the sixteenth century the miners who dug coal after the style of the monks of Newbattle had only scratched the surface of the nation's wealth.

A gold coin of James VI as king of England, Ireland, Scotland and Wales. It reads : I would make them one people.

17 SEVENTEENTH CENTURY

A courtier, Robert Carey, rode north from London in 1603 to tell James VI of Queen Elizabeth's death. People marvelled at the speed of his journey, because he covered the 640 kilometres in only sixty hours.

Nowadays the journey by air from London to Edinburgh takes sixty minutes. Living, working and travelling in seventeenth-century Scotland was still very different from what it is today.

The sketches made by John Slezer in 1693 show the differences very clearly. They picture a land of naked hills and rough moorland, with tiny burghs clustered round old churches and castles. The roads that link the burghs are only rough tracks.

Scotland was still a land of country folk. Ninety per cent of the population were peasant farmers, living in one-roomed hovels built with their own hands, wearing clothes of homespun wool and linen.

The central lowlands were the richest area, with wheat, oats and barley grown in the Lothians and Clydesdale, dairy farming in Ayrshire and fruit-growing in the sheltered Clyde valley. Edinburgh and Glasgow, market towns as well as centres for spinning and weaving, were the two largest burghs.

John Slezer was a Dutchman serving in Scotland as a captain in the army. His book of sketches 'Theatrum Scotiae' was published in 1693.

Slezer's view of Dumbarton Rock. Sportsmen are fowling and fishing by the Clyde. The only buildings in sight are the ancient castle on the Rock and a couple of farm cottages.

Slezer shows a peaceful farming scene at Brechin, countryfolk leading a laden horse. The field is ridged with wide plough furrows beginning to be overgrown by weeds and scrub.

Women washing clothes at Dundee, a sight to be seen in any part of Scotland. Two are stamping out the dirt with their bare feet – which, in winter, would be blue with cold.

Bride and bridegroom lead the dancing in De Wit's painting of a Lowland Wedding (1684). The men wear flat bonnets, long coats and breeches while the women have plaids over their heads and shoulders. The man in the right foreground sports a large basket-hilted sword.

On both the east and west coasts there were herring ports, Greenock on the west and Anstruther, Crail and Dunbar on the east. Musselburgh and Leith were famous for shell-fish and oysters.

Coal was mined along the Forth, round Glasgow and at Irvine, and was used for the salt pans at Saltcoats and Prestonpans, as well as for glass making, soap boiling and other small industries in the burghs.

The Border lands were less populated, for the great sheep farms needed fewer workers, and in Galloway much land was given over to horse and cattle breeding. Dumfries, Wigtown, Peebles and the old Border towns of Jedburgh, Kelso and Melrose were the chief centres, while Portpatrick linked the south-west area with Ireland.

Some of Slezer's drawings show lowlanders at their daily work, farmers in their fields, herdsmen with cattle and sheep, women at their wash tubs, fishermen netting salmon and packmen leading laden horses. Others show comfortable-

Three men hunting duck at Culross. One shoots, one collects the fallen birds and a third sits comfortably smoking a churchwarden pipe, with a boathook for birds that fall in the water.

Nobles hunting deer in the Duke of Hamilton's Low Park. A full century was to pass before coal mines and ironworks made Lanarkshire an industrial area.

looking burgesses enjoying an afternoon at fishing and fowling.

Another drawing shows high life in the Duke of Hamilton's parks. For most people shooting had taken the place of deer hunting but the greatest aristocrats still had their deer parks. Wearing plumed hats, flowing coats and long riding boots, they ride at a stag chased up by hounds and beater.

Yet another drawing shows an assembly of nobility at a great country mansion. The gentlemen wear wigs and low-crowned hats, long many-buttoned coats, kneebreeches and ribboned shoes. They carry swords as a sign of their rank. The ladies wear long dresses with panniers and elbow-length sleeves, long curls and little caps.

The courtyard is full of private coaches. Wealthy people liked having a private coach to show off their wealth though they could only use it when the roads were dry, in the summer.

Working people dressed more plainly, even on festive occasions, in clothes made from homespun linen and wool.

An aristocratic gathering at Thirlestane Castle outside Lauder, Berwick. The garden is formal in the French style and the costume is that of the nobility and the wealthy.

Private carriages at Falkland, Fife. Slezer makes the big coaches look attractive but they had no springs and the almost impassable roads soon shattered wheels and axles.

De Wit's Highland Wedding shows the guests dressed much the same as in the Lowland Wedding, except that the men are wearing tartan trews.

Three methods of transporting goods : packhorse, back-pack and bundle. All three travellers are carrying stout walking sticks. In the background of Slezer's picture is Culross Abbey.

Slezer's pictures do not include the highlands. Beyond the highland line there were no roads and no towns. The highlanders lived a separate way of life in their bleak and mountainous country: hunting, fishing, grazing sheep and cattle, and tilling their small stony fields. The Gaelic-speaking clansmen travelled long distances to markets at Inverness, Perth, Dunkeld and Crieff.

South-east of the highland line life was more varied. The flat lands round Inverness, the Black Isle, and the plains of Moray and Aberdeen provided good farming land, such as the lands about the Tay. Here harvests ripened quickly and farmers grew enough to sell their grain to other parts of Scotland as well as to the

Continent. Aberdeen and Dundee had grown into big ports of over 10 000 people. Aberdeen had a prosperous woollen industry and Dundee, like Perth and Montrose, was a centre for the linen trade. Both the Don and the Tay were salmon-fishing rivers.

One of Slezer's most interesting views is a sketch of Scotland's biggest seventeenth-century city, Edinburgh. It shows how the farm rigs go right up to the waters of the North Loch, where Edinburgh's Princes Street and Gardens lie today.

The sketch was made from the village of Dean, now swallowed up in central Edinburgh and overlaid with houses. Slezer saw it as a hamlet on the Water of Leith, a jumble of stone houses and cottages set among gardens and haystacks. Down at the water's edge a double water wheel worked a waulk mill, where cloth was finished off and felted.

Edinburgh was already facing a problem of overcrowding. The burgh now filled the long rocky ridge stretching from the Castle to the Netherbow Port and the population was packed into steep wynds branching like herring bones from the High Street, as can be seen in an old map of 1647.

To house more people builders raised tenements up to eleven storeys high but usually of six or seven storeys. Rich and poor lived in the same block.

The best houses were two or three storeys up, well away from the noise and dirt of the streets but not too far to climb. Rich lawyers or nobles lived in these. Shopkeepers and craftsmen lived above, and poor people on the ground level or in the cellars.

Slezer's view of Edinburgh and the village of Dean on the Water of Leith. A watermill was built nearby in the time of David I and successive mills stood on the spot till recently.

John Slezer's job was to inspect armouries and powder magazines. His sketch of Edinburgh Castle shows a soldier's grasp of the fortifications of the castle.

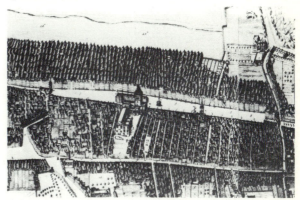

This old map, 1647, shows how the seventeenth-century burgh of Edinburgh now consisted of a solid mass of housing on each side of the High Street.

The painting by Roderick Chambers of the Craftsmen of Holyroodhouse Palace, 1721, shows each carrying out his special task. Reading from left to right : sievewright, slater, glazier, cooper, mason, wright, bowmaker, painter, plumber and upholsterer.

Some lawyers and burgesses lived in the Cowgate or Westerbow areas, which they could reach by horse and carriage. Even there they were content with a house of three rooms and a kitchen. Lord Kennet was a famous lawyer but at night his children and their nurse slept in his study, and the maidservant slept under a cupboard in the kitchen. The other two rooms were the lawyer's bedroom and the drawing room.

By 1690 the Burgh Council bought up other lands to build on. These included the neighbouring burgh of Canongate and also High Riggs, the Pleasance, North Leith and Portsburgh.

Seventeenth-century builders had no idea of sanitation and visitors to Edin-burgh learned to dread the sound of the Town drum at ten o'clock. This was the signal for women to tip sewage and slops out of the upstairs windows, with a warning shout of 'Gardyloo'.

Pedestrians shouted: 'Haud your haund!' or dived for shelter, but nothing could stop the terrible and deadly stench known as 'the flowers of Edinburgh'.

In 1687 the Council hired twenty two-horse carts to take away refuse every night except Sunday. The filth often contaminated the water supply and water from the wells contained a murderous collection of germs.

Few of Edinburgh's 30 000 residents were burgesses. Many people worked as porters, water carriers, milk vendors,

Canongate burgh immediately below Edinburgh (see the map on page 85) was much less crowded. Many houses still had large gardens.

Wealthy merchants such as Heriot and the Hutchesons left money to help orphans of members of the Guild. Above: Heriot's School today.

A street view of Paul's Work which was a large building enclosing an inner courtyard. The Town Council and private individuals supported it with their money – for a while.

Napier's Bones: the first calculating machine, invented by John Napier (1550–1617) who also invented logarithms. The two inventions led eventually to the modern slide rule.

hawkers, drovers, carters, servants, sedan chairmen, labourers or link-boys – who carried torches and guided people through the dark streets.

An early eighteenth-century visitor, Captain Burt, described the Edinburgh caddies (porters and guides) as 'wretches that lie in rags upon the streets'.

When they could get no work the poor lived on charity. The Town Council gave licences allowing people to beg and opened a Poor House, Paul's Work, in 1633. Kirk Sessions also collected alms and doled them out to the poor.

Members of the Guilds looked after their own poor, for every member paid a contribution to Guild Funds. Rich merchants such as George Heriot left money to found hospitals (orphanages) for the orphan children of burgesses.

When Daniel Defoe (journalist and author of *Robinson Crusoe*) visited Edinburgh in 1707 he reported it was as bad as London for shoplifters, house-robbers and pickpockets, even though it had a Town Guard of two companies of armed and uniformed watchmen.

Seventeenth-century painting of Lady Mary Erskine by George Jamesone (born in Aberdeen 1587). She wears a lace collar, starched ruff and dress with elaborate sleeves.

Self portrait by seventeenth-century painter Scougal shows the fashion of the day : carefully trimmed moustache, clipped beard and dark clothing with white collar and cuffs.

Daniel Defoe thought Edinburgh a fine city, in spite of its dirt and smell. He compared its beautiful stone buildings with the 'paper-built' cities of England and especially admired its High Street, 'the longest and best-built' in Europe.

The centre of city life was the Market Cross, where the trumpeter regularly blew for silence and the herald read out public announcements. The Cross was busiest between eleven and one o'clock, for merchants, lawyers and other gentlemen gathered in the open to discuss business and politics and the news of the day.

Women shopped for herbs, fruit and vegetables in the open market held every morning in the High Street. For other goods they went to the special walled markets, the Meal Market, Flesh Market, Poultry Market or Butter Market. Once a week they could buy drapery, woollens and linen cloth in the Landmarket. Rich people who wanted luxury goods ordered them from the merchants who had warehouses full of goods in the West Bow, and who supplied all the tradesmen's needs in the way of timber, iron goods, paint, oil, dyes, drugs and so on.

When he visited Glasgow in the same year, Defoe found it 'one of the cleanliest, most beautiful and best built cities in Great Britain'. It had been rebuilt after a fire in 1677 with wide streets and stone houses all planned the same size. The lower storeys rested on arched columns,

Another view of the Old Bridge, Glasgow – it can be compared with the picture on page 61. This was the only bridge until the Broomielaw was built late in the eighteenth century.

A seventeenth-century lowland woman, with long skirt, linen apron, short cloak and starched collar. The sober costume almost certainly reflects the influence of the Kirk.

Solid seventeenth-century houses with outside forestairs line Castle Street, Glasgow. Beyond rises the Cathedral tower. The costume of the woman at the market stall and of the pedestrians shows that the picture was not made until the early nineteenth century.

providing space for booths and market stalls.

Glasgow had the reputation of being the godliest city in Scotland. Its Church organisation gives us a good idea of how the Kirk ruled people's lives in other burghs also.

The Reformed Church was modelled on John Calvin's Church in Geneva. Ministers in Glasgow wanted to build up a god-fearing community and worked hand in glove with the magistrates to make sure that citizens lived sober and upright lives.

The cathedral was taken over to house Presbyterian congregations. The choir became the Inner High Kirk, the nave the Outer High Kirk and the crypt the Laigh or Barony Kirk. Rows of stones served as seats in the great cavernous building, until wooden forms were provided for the men. Women were expected to bring their own folding stools.

The Arch-Prelate of St Andrewes in Scotland reading the new Service-booke in his pontificalibus assaulted by men & women, with Cricketts stooles Stickes and Stones.

When Charles I, and later Charles II, tried to model the Scottish Kirk on the Church of England, people were very angry. This drawing shows the 'Arch Prelate' of St. Andrews being attacked while in the pulpit. Many noblemen and their followers signed the National Covenant in 1638, declaring their support for the Scottish Kirk.

RANGE OF HOUSES IN CASTLE STREET, OPPOSITE THE BARONY CHURCH, PARTLY TAKEN DOWN IN 1844.

The Low Corner House was the Hangman's Abode.   Prebendal Manse of the Lord of Provan.

Rotten Row, Glasgow. A prebendal manse was a house owned by a large city church and occupied by one of its ministers. Wealthy men sometimes gave a house to the Kirk.

The ministers preached long sermons, often terrifying the congregation by describing how God would punish the wicked. Sometimes they were not so fiery and people dozed off. Beadles had orders to use their long sticks to lift women's headshawls to make sure that they stayed awake.

In the reign of Charles I the whole country rose in rebellion when the king tried to change the Scottish Kirk to match the Church of England.

After the Civil War the ministers and magistrates punished Sabbath-breaking very severely. Women must not gossip or draw water from the well in service time. No buying or selling was allowed. Ministers and elders scolded those lingering after the service to gossip by the bridge and Seizers arrested idle strollers. The schoolmaster had orders to punish boys found playing outdoors.

Respectable families attended kirk twice a day, ate a cold dinner in silence and then sat in a darkened room. Shutters were opened to give just enough light for reading the Scriptures.

Absentees from church had to pay fines or stand dressed only in a sackcloth robe at the pillar of repentance.

The Kirk disapproved of Christmas festivities and Glasgow Kirk Session speedily banned the custom of pipers touring the streets on St. Thomas's Eve (22 December). They also forbade all Christmas plays, guisings, pipings, drink and other 'superstitious exercises'.

They also kept a severe eye on people's private behaviour. They scolded husbands and wives who quarrelled, frowned on dancing, piping and drumming at weddings and christenings, and they appointed 'Noters' who reported those who swore or blasphemed. The fine was twelve pence.

Kirk Sessions had the right to punish misbehaviour in all sorts of ways. There were penances, when the offender stood at the Church door or by a pillar, barefooted, often wearing a white sheet with a paper fastened on their brows to show what they were guilty of. Kirk Sessions sometimes fined culprits or ordered them to be put in the jougs or branks, or sent them to the Correction House in Rotten Row, to be fed on bread and water and whipped daily.

Slezer's view of Haddington shows the rough track which was the main road through to Edinburgh, the unfenced rigs and the huge church, the 'Lamp of Lothian'.

Presbyterian reformers and their congregations disapproved of the decorated churches of the Middle Ages. Lyne Church, near Peebles, is built in the plain post-Reformation style.

Two forms of punishment. Left: jougs — an iron neck ring attached to a pillar. Right: branks — an iron cage which could be fitted round the head and over the tongue.

A banner carried by Covenanters in 1679: they had made a 'covenant' (promise) to God, to uphold what they believed to be the true faith.

The Kirk kept up this kind of control over people's lives right into the eighteenth century, particularly in the southwest. Charles II (1660–85) appointed bishops and took away the right of congregations to elect their own ministers. Three hundred ministers gave up their kirks and held open-air services, coventicles, rather than obey. They risked torture and death and so did the congregations who supported them. Sentries were posted to give warning of the approach of the king's troops.

The Covenanters, as the rebels were called, were ready to fight if necessary. In June 1679 a group of armed Lanarkshire farmers defeated a troop of professional

In 1679 a group of Lanarkshire and Ayrshire farmers (40 mounted and 200 on foot) defeated a larger force of dragoons at Drumclog, near Strathaven, Lanark. (This success encouraged Covenanters to resist a royal army at Bothwell Brig. But there they ran out of ammunition and were defeated.)

soldiers led by Graham of Claverhouse at Drumclog.

The persecution of Covenanters ended when William and Mary became rulers in 1690 and the Presbyterian Church set up again under the rule of its General Assembly.

At times the strong religious feeling of the seventeenth century led to hideous crimes. The Scots were the worst persecutors of supposed witches in the whole of Europe – over 4000 died in witch-hunts in the seventeenth and early eighteenth centuries.

Persecution went on until 1728, when the last execution of a 'witch' took place at Dornoch and an old woman was strangled on a charge of having turned her daughter into a pony. By that time educated people had lost their fear of witchcraft and as more people learned to read their belief in spells and magic died away.

The spread of education was due to the Kirk, which set great store on every person being able to read the word of God set down in the Bible. As early as 1560 the Scots reformers had published a plan for a network of schools and colleges in 'The Book of Discipline' which said that there should be a school in every parish.

In 1696 the Scottish parliament passed an Act which said landowners and tenants had to pay a stent and provide a school in each parish. They also had to appoint a schoolmaster and pay him a salary of 100 marks (£5.11s) a year.

This was a very low salary, even though the children also paid a small fee every quarter. Schoolmasters had to do other work to eke out their incomes. They acted as parish clerks, precentors and sometimes even as gravediggers.

People accused of witchcraft had little chance of escape. Many were tortured till they confessed.

Swimming a witch: anyone guilty would float.

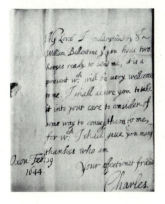

An example of the handwriting of the time. A letter written by Charles II, as 14 year old Prince of Wales, to the Duke of Roxburghe, thanking him for the present of two horses.

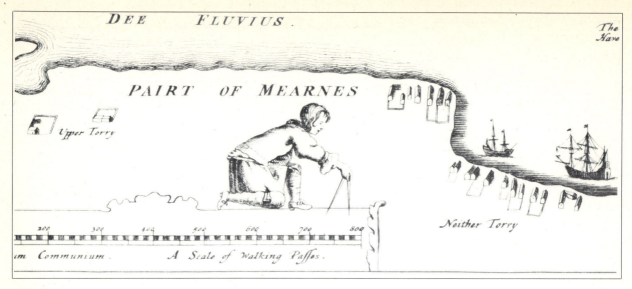

A detail from a map of Aberdeen by James Gordon, 1661. It was quite usual for maps to have illustrations on them, or to have a decorative border. Such illustrations give a good idea of life at the time. Here a kilted schoolboy kneels to use his compasses or dividers – as many children had to do when there was no furniture.

Farmers were often so poor themselves that they had no money for the teacher's salary and had to pay him in oatmeal instead. Often the poor schoolmaster had to trudge all round the parish to collect it.

There were no proper schools and classes met in barns and byres and old sheds. Sometimes the children lay on their stomachs and used the floor as a desk, and in other schools they took it in turn to sit at the table and benches. Even so, Scotland was ahead of the other countries of Europe in having a national school system at all and during the eighteenth century most lowland Scottish boys and girls learned to read and write.

Burgh schools flourished as Scotland's overseas trade increased and merchants wanted education for their sons. To become a member of a merchant guild a boy already had to serve a five-year apprenticeship in the arts of commerce and go overseas with a cargo at least three times.

Ships from Edinburgh, Dundee and Aberdeen traded regularly with Trondheim, Danzig, Rotterdam and Veere in the north and La Rochelle, Bordeaux and Spain in the south.

By 1690, however, Scottish merchants began to feel a grievance against their English neighbours. English merchants were growing rich through trade with their colonies in the West Indies and America but Scottish merchants were not allowed to trade there.

In 1695 they formed a trading company and tried to set up a colony of their own, at Darien, on the narrow strip of land between North and South America. Burgesses all over the lowlands invested money in the scheme and looked forward to new prosperity. It was a terrible shock when the scheme failed. Darien was unhealthy, the colonists were struck down by malaria, there was no sale for their goods and they were attacked by

Gladstone's Land, an old merchant's house in Edinburgh's Lawnmarket. The booth (shop) would have been on ground level with the outside staircase leading to the house above.

The Merchants' House, Glasgow, headquarters of the Merchants' Guild, was founded in 1601 and rebuilt in 1659, a sign of the merchants' prosperity. Only the tower remains. A carving above the door is shown on page 77.

Spaniards. In 1700 they abandoned the colony, bitter because the English gave them no help.

Already there had been trouble in the highlands, where the MacDonalds had been massacred in 1692 on orders from the government at Westminster. It only needed another misfortune to make the Scots wish to break away from the union which had begun when James VI took the English crown.

The coat of arms of the company which wanted to establish a trading centre at Darien (Panama). The failure of the scheme hit all Scottish merchants very badly. ➤

The second Duke of Queensberry (son of the builder of Drumlanrig Castle) worked very astutely to prepare the Act of Union 1707. Here he presents the Act to Queen Anne.

Gold unit (James VI) reverse on page 80.

Silver thirty-shilling piece (Charles I)

Silver two-merk piece (Charles II)

PRE-UNION COINS

Copper bawbee (William and Mary) with thistle reverse.

18 THE ACT OF UNION

Fresh disaster came between 1695 and 1702 with seven years of famine. The weather was so bad that farmers could not harvest until January or February. Summers brought nothing but rain, heavy frosts came down in early autumn and blizzards and deep snowdrifts followed in the winter.

In some parishes over one-third of the people died of hunger and others survived only by eating weeds, docks and wild spinach – and even snails. It was a time of 'blue faces and clean teeth' and landlords had no money to help their tenants.

Feeling against England ran so high that the English government feared that Scotland would break away and become a separate country under its own ruler. The Scots might even ally with England's enemy, France.

To stop this it suggested that Scotland should give up its Parliament and join with other parts of Britain with full rights to trade with England and her colonies. This big common market would help to build up Scottish prosperity. In 1707 the Act of Union joined the countries together.

Under the Act of Union Scotland gave

The Old Pretender, 'James VIII', father of ► Bonnie Prince Charlie, landing at Peterhead in January 1716 to encourage the ill-organised Jacobite Rebellion (the 'Fifteen') against George I.

up its Parliament at Edinburgh and agreed to send 45 Members to the House of Commons in London. Scottish lords chose 16 peers to represent them in the House of Lords.

Scotland kept its own laws and Presbyterian Church and its own system of education but coinage, weights and measures were to be common. A new flag, the Union Jack, was designed to include the cross of St. Andrew and the crosses of St. George and St. David.

It was some years before the Union began to bring real prosperity to the country, for at first the small Scottish industries could not compete with the large English trading companies. There were troubles also because the Jacobites wished to replace the German-born king George I by descendants of the House of Stewart.

In 1715 the Jacobites of Scotland and northern England began a rebellion to put James VII's son, James Stewart, on the throne as James VIII. Though it put down the rebellion easily enough the British government had to pay closer attention to what was happening in the distant north, where the clansmen still spoke their ancient Gaelic tongue and followed their own customs.

'The March of George I's Forces and Cannon to ► Perth' 1715. Moving the royal cannon northward took a long time – to judge from the number of horses yoked to the cannon and from the activity of the engineers clearing a road.

EIGHTEENTH CENTURY: Effects of Union

Kenneth Sutherland, Lord Duffus, in highland dress, about 1700. He wears a slashed doublet and linen shirt with a belted plaid which serves as 'kilt' and cloak combined.

Highlanders wearing the plaid in various ways: one part of the long strip of cloth forms a 'kilt', the rest is slung over one shoulder or pulled over both shoulders as a cloak.

19 Eighteenth Century: HIGHLANDS

The highland chiefs had lost some of their power in the seventeenth century but they were still the most important men in the north. Their clansmen revered them, and did their bidding without a murmur. Chiefs still ruled the countryside through their private law courts and in the wilder parts they still had power of life and death over their people.

Even in the eighteenth century chiefs were still warlords, and they counted their wealth in the number of fighting men they could call upon in time of need.

Many still encouraged their tenants to carry on the old sport of cattle lifting and took a share of the spoils. Some, like MacDonell of Barisdale, offered 'protection' from robbers: farmers paid 'blackmail' so that their cattle would not be stolen. MacDonell made £500 a year in this way.

Next in rank were the chief's relatives, *tacksmen*, who paid the chief a small rent for estates and then rented land out to the

An old droving route through the heart of the highlands. Animals had to be taken to market live – there was no means of transport.

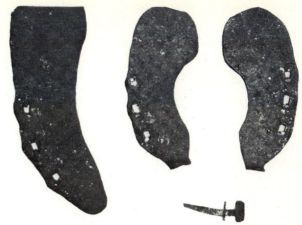

Cattle shoes were made for centuries. Those on the right were made by smiths in a Perthshire village about 1865.

Cattle being driven through the shallow waters of the Solway Firth.

lesser tenants and sub-tenants. Chiefs and tacksmen were the warleaders of the clan, owners of the biggest herds of black cattle.

Cattle-rearing was an important part of the highland way of life. Clansmen and chief alike depended on selling cattle at Trysts held at Crieff and elsewhere. The beasts were small (25–30 stone as against modern cattle averaging 64–88 stone) but hardy, and they cost nothing to transport. After the Trysts they were fitted with special shoes and driven south to the markets of England.

A visitor to Crieff in 1723 described the appearance of the chiefs and their followers, armed to the teeth:

> The highland gentlemen were mighty civil, dressed in their slashed waistcoats and trousing (which is breeches and stocking in one piece of striped stuff) with a plaid for a cloak and a blue bonnet. They have a poiniard, knife and fork in one sheath hanging at one side of their belt, their pistol at the other and their snuffmill before, with a great broadsword at their side. Their attendance was very numerous, all in belted plaids, girt like women's petticoats down to the knee, leaving thighs and half the leg all bare. They had also each a broadsword and a poiniard.

Field Marshal Lord George Wade 1673–1748. Here he is in armour but he usually wore the long coat and breeches shown on page 97. He earned more fame building roads and bridges than by fighting. The bridge, his finest, is over the Tay at Aberfeldy.

The Government in London was much alarmed by the Rebellion of 1715 and by tales of disorder, robbery, cattle rustling and blackmail that reached London. In 1724 it sent General Wade to Inverness as Commander-in-Chief, to keep the highlands quiet.

Wade quickly recruited six Highland Companies, to patrol the mountain passes and distant glens. Then he collected in illegal weapons from the clansmen and began to build roads. These were to link the garrisons at Fort William, Fort Augustus and Fort George (Inverness).

The road made a route now followed by the A82 and B852 and was finished in 1728. Wade then set 300 men to work on a road to Dunkeld.

Captains and lieutenants supervised the road building. Serjeants became foremen and privates provided the labour. Each day they worked on the road the officers got 2/6d, the serjeants and skilled tradesmen got 1/–d, corporals and drummers 8d, and privates 6d.

Letters written by Captain Burt, one of Wade's staff officers, are our best guide to highland life at the time.

Highland shielings on Jura: the shielings (rather like Indian wigwams covered in wattle) were used as temporary homes during the summer grazing season in upland pastures.

He was greatly surprised at the difference in appearance between chiefs and tacksmen, on the one hand, and the ordinary people. 'The gentry may be said to be a handsome people', he wrote, 'but the commonalty much otherwise; one would hardly think by their faces that they were the same species.'

The difference was due to bad food, exposure to weather and the everlasting reek of peat fires. In the long winters much time was spent sheltering from the weather and the smoke yellowed the skin and inflamed the eyes.

The poverty horrified the captain, when he saw the tiny amounts of goods brought for sale at the Inverness fair: a small roll of linen, a piece of plaiding, a pound or two of cheese or butter or a few goatskins.

The costume also worried him. He described the men as half naked, dressed in a large plaid girded to form a combined kilt and cloak. At least they wore brogues. Women went barefoot, in the coldest weather. In fishing towns he watched, amazed, as they carried their husbands ashore from the boats.

Women carry their husbands (with laden creels) from fishing boats in the early century.

S.W. Prospect of the CASTLE,
at Inverness.

The view that
travellers saw as
they approached
Inverness from the
south-west in the
early eighteenth
century. The castle
was blown up by the
Jacobite forces
before the Battle of
Culloden.

Inverness was the chief trading town of the north. Burt describes it as a town of 'four streets', a tiny place, and its shops and warehouses were poorly stocked.

Houses, as in other burghs along the Moray Firth, were built Dutch-style, with their backs to the street and a courtyard reached through an alleyway. Living quarters were reached by an outside stair, and the ground floor used as warehouse or shop. It was only in the great burghs that builders used properly squared stone. In Inverness and elsewhere houses were built of rubble and the walls made homes for thousands of rats, their nests hidden by the harling on the outside of the walls.

The gentry, bailies and shopkeepers all dressed English-style and spoke English as well as Gaelic or 'Irish', as Burt calls it. Gaelic was the only language spoken by most people in the north and west as far south as Loch Lomond.

Shopkeepers were well-off and could afford two or three maidservants. The poor girls were fed on oatmeal and paid three half crowns a year. Every moment of their 'spare' time was spent spinning for their mistress.

Captain Burt's journeys often took him on journeys beyond Inverness. He met highland chiefs with retinues of haunchman, piper, spokesman and numerous gillies – each gillie had a special task. One led the chief's horse over precipitous country, another looked after the baggage and another crossed before when the chief forded a flooded stream.

Burt describes one October journey in detail. He rode on horseback, a bag of lemons at the saddlebow for making brandy punch and a second horse carrying his portmanteau. His guide padded along on foot.

They crossed the first river on an ancient

Women sitting by a long trough sing as they felt home-woven cloth with their bare feet. A young man in bonnet and plaid leans on a staff – apparently doing nothing.

This picture of a mounted officer (detail from an engraving of the Battle of Culloden 1746) gives an idea of Captain Burt's appearance.

ferry boat sixty years old, patched with rough timber. The oars were held in place by the highlander's favourite twine, twisted birch roots.

The second obstacle was a peat bog, where the captain in his heavy boots broke through and the packhorse sank up to its neck.

He tackled another river by riding through it, practising the skill of fixing his eyes on the opposite bank and ignoring the rushing water. On another occasion he inched his way across two slender pine trees which formed a bridge and dragged the horse along by its reins.

Women grind corn, using a pivoted stick to rotate the quern (see pages 5 and 107).

Slezer at Kelso: horse ferry over the Tweed. Elsewhere, horses often had to swim rivers.

EIGHTEENTH CENTURY: A highland journey

Flora Macdonald from South Uist was jailed for smuggling Prince Charles to Skye disguised as her maid. She later spent 30 years in America.

An imaginary picture of Charles with Antoine Walsh on the shore of Loch Nan Uamh, Inverness, having landed from a French ship, August 1745. In fact he usually wore trews.

Private, 92nd Gordon Highlanders 1815. When highland dress was later revived among civilians, it copied the military style.

At night they reached a small clachan and Burt went into the farmer's house while another hut was made ready for his night's stay.

The floor was soft earth with metre-high walls made of wattles packed on the outside with turf. A framework of naturally crooked timbers held up the heavy roof beam whose weight helped to stop the house being blown away during gales.

The wife and family of naked children squatted round a central peat fire. When Burt's eyes began to smart he went outside to dodge the smoke. He was amazed to see smoke pouring out of the roof, ribs and door of his own lodging, so that it looked like a steaming dung hill.

Once the newly lit peats had burned down to a steady glow, he found his quarters very comfortable. Sheets and blankets were spotlessly clean and, best of all, there were no bugs or fleas.

He could not eat the meat offered to him and, as usual, had boiled eggs instead.

A highland clachan at Loch Doich, Wester Ross, in 1880. Highland dwellings had changed little since the days when Captain Burt rode past in the early eighteenth century.

Like most visitors to the north, he found it hard to get used to highland cooking.

The Jacobites used Wade's roads in their dash for Edinburgh in 1745. The '45 was much less dangerous than it seemed, however. Many clan leaders had no wish for a Stewart on the throne and gave no help to Prince Charles Edward, 'Bonnie Prince Charlie'.

The clansmen who fought at Culloden followed their chiefs as heroically and devotedly as ever. Their defeat really marks the end of the old highland way of life all over the north and west. The government at once passed severe laws banning the kilt and bagpipe and the carrying of weapons. It also confiscated the lands of rebel chiefs and took them under government control, and put an end to the private law courts of all highland lords.

During the next thirty years government trustees spent the rents from the forfeited estates improving life for the highland people, building roads, bridges and

Burt stayed in houses like this during his travels. A pot hangs from the ceiling over a peat fire burning on a central hearth.

schools.

Chiefs encouraged young men to join the new Highland Regiments (they got £3 for every recruit) and highlanders fought Britain's wars in Europe and North America. The government in London was sure of highland loyalty by 1782. It ended the laws against highland dress and pipes and allowed the chiefs to return to their estates.

The Bear Gates at Traquair House, Peebles, built 1737–8. Four gallons of ale were provided for the workmen who erected them. According to one tradition, the 5th Earl of Traquair, a staunch Jacobite, closed the main gates in 1745 after saying farewell to Prince Charles and vowed that they would not be re-opened until the Stuart kings were restored to the throne. They are still kept closed today.

A concealed portrait of Prince Charles: the artist painted the features on the wooden base but they are visible as a recognisable face only in the reflection glass, when looked at from the right direction.

The thirty years of peace ended the old highland way of life. Chiefs no longer fostered sons out, to live among fellow clansmen, to learn Gaelic and to make friends among the people. They now hired lowland tutors or sent their sons south to learn English ways. When they grew up, landowners of the new generation thought highland customs ridiculous and did their best to change them. Chiefs who had spent thirty years in exile in Holland, France and Germany did not remember how their clansmen had suffered at Culloden. They were interested only in the income that their rents would bring.

The tacksmen found that they were no longer needed or respected. Chiefs did not need fighting men now and asked the tacksmen to pay higher rents. Many tacksmen were too proud to stay where they were no longer needed. They emigrated to America, sometimes taking their tenants with them and setting up clans of their own in the New World.

People found it harder to pay higher rents, for the population grew rapidly in the late eighteenth century and farms became smaller with each new generation.

Already many people had left the islands and highlands, driven out by starvation. Hundreds of poor people in Skye lived just like the *strand loopers* of the Middle Stone Age, eating little except limpets and shell-fish.

Thousands of highlanders moved to the lowland towns in search of work and others emigrated to North Carolina and Canada.

Many highland families were saved from starvation by growing potatoes which became their main food supply. To pay

A twentieth-century photograph of one of the oldest thatched cottages on South Uist. They still rely on heavy stones to hold on the thatch, but modern wire netting is more effective than ropes.

'Town Guard' by David Allan (1744–1796). Many guards were highlanders, taking work in towns.

Grinding corn in Skye in the nineteenth century by the old method.

their rents and buy necessities they could not grow on the farm – iron tools, leather, salt and needles – they depended on selling cattle to the drovers who toured the glens each year. Fresh meat was needed for English towns and to supply the navy with salt beef. Britain was at war with either France or Spain for most of the eighteenth century and the Napoleonic Wars lasted till 1815.

Landowners with a quick eye for profit soon realised that sheep, which supplied both wool and meat, brought bigger profits than cattle. Sheep could also survive better on the short grass of hillsides.

In 1762 the graziers from the Borders rented pastures in Argyll, Dumbartonshire and Perthshire; and soon looked for more land in Ross-shire and Sutherland.

This drawing records a common sight of the early nineteenth century, a ship waiting for for highland families forced to emigrate because they had been evicted from their crofts.

Left : black-faced highland sheep have curling horns and long coarse fleece. They are hardy, good mutton and providers of excellent wool for tweed manufacture. Right : great Cheviot sheep 'ate up' the highlands. White-faced, hornless, they provide a medium-weight wool free from dark streaks. Heads and upper legs have no thick wool.

Sheep-farming brought disaster to the highland peasants. There was no room on the hillsides for black cattle and soft-fleeced highland sheep once the herds of big white Cheviot and Black Face Linton sheep arrived. As the sheep moved in the people had to move out.

Others left because they were driven out when their old chiefs, the landowners, decided to rent out the land for sheep grazing. Sheep farmers could pay twenty times more rent than the peasant farmers. Landowners gave their tenants notice to quit, tore down houses and farm build-ings and turned farms into pasture.

These 'Clearances' brought great sad-ness and bitterness. People did not wish to leave the glens where their ancestors had lived for centuries. One of the worst Clearances took place in Sutherland where 15 000 people were turned off.

People who did not move quickly enough were brutally driven out, as in Strathnaver (Sutherland) in 1819. The factor offered them land on the coast, so that they could set up as fishermen, but they had no boats, no money and no experience. It was a miserable exchange.

At Dunfermline, Slezer saw thatched cottages, barns and conical haystacks enclosed by a neat wall – probably built of stones from the old abbey. Transport is the same as on page 84.

Wide unfenced fields near Arbroath. The farm-workers are followed by a man with a horse and sled. Sledges were in common use because trackways were too rough for cart wheels.

20 Eighteenth Century: LOWLANDS

When Daniel Defoe visited Scotland after the Union he found it foreign in every way. In his 'Tour of Great Britain' he described how the moment he crossed the Border an icy 'Scots gale' made him cover his eyes and dismount from his horse, in case he was blown off.

He marvelled at the bleak wastes of Coldingham Moor and the lack of trees. Even the food was different. The herrings at Dunbar were red in colour, cured differently from those of Yarmouth and he found one delicacy, a Soland goose, impossible to eat because it tasted of fish. (A Soland 'goose' is a gannet.)

Sometimes he admired what he saw, but he thought farming methods were backward and the soil impoverished. The tenanted farms were still divided into rigs and worked jointly by the tenants and cottars of the farm-touns. The poorest cottars struggled to keep alive by working as paid labourers and by growing oats on a small patch of ground.

Scottish landowners who journeyed to England also saw differences between the two countries. In particular they looked at the prosperous English farms and decided to change matters at home.

On Roy's map of East Lothian (1750s) some rigs are shown already enclosed to make farms that landlords could rent to single tenants.

Men digging in a field near Glasgow. The tree-lined road later became Argyle Street. The view includes the Cathedral on the left and Bishop Rae's Old Bridge on the right.

Already at the end of the seventeenth century wealthy landowners were planting trees in their own parklands, as Slezer shows in this view of Argile House.

Portobello, near Edinburgh, was a village that grew up because of fine clay deposits, used for bricks and for white stoneware. Coloured figurines and pots were prized possessions.

Their improvements were to change the look of the Scottish countryside. They enclosed fields with hedges and ditches and planted new crops, clover and turnips, to enrich the soil and to provide feed for cattle in the winter. They also encouraged farmers to follow the English pattern of growing turnips, peas, oats and clover in turn.

Above all they planted trees. Most of the plantations, copses and woods of today were started by the tree-planting landowners. The Earl of Loudon planted a million trees in Ayrshire, the Earl of Stair planted 20 000 trees a year in Wigtown. The Earl of Atholl planted new sorts of trees as well as old, millions of fir, oak, elm, ash, walnut, beech, laburnum as well as larch trees which he brought in from the Tyrol in Austria.

The improved farms brought more profits to the landlords and better food to the tenants. Potatoes, turnips and sometimes beef or mutton helped out their old diet.

With more money available tea-drinking became popular. Some people thought that tea-drinking was bad for the health and others advised that a little whisky was

Teaset c. 1790 in the Dumfries Burgh Museum. Tea drinking came from China – and Chinese teacups today are often made without handles.

needed in the last cup to cancel out the bad effects of the tea. Old-fashioned ministers preached against both tea and whisky as equally bad for the drinker. In the towns, bakers began to specialise in the tea-breads and pastries that go so well with tea-drinking.

Other signs of prosperity appeared in farmers' houses at the end of the century. Ministers who wrote about their parishes for the first Statistical Account of 1790 describe how nearly ever farmer's house now had an eight-day clock and every farm servant a watch. These were still very precious possessions, carefully handed down from father to eldest son.

A grandfather clock made in Dumfries 1745. The mechanism is worked by weights and a pendulum inside the tall case. The clockfaces of such clocks were decorated in various ways, some being gilded and others painted in different colours to show scenes of country life.

Woodhead Farm: an early eighteenth-century lowland farm, home of the Baird family of Gartsherrie.

High Cross Farm to which the Bairds moved in 1808. The new house is tiled, not thatched, and the walls are built of dressed stone.

An Edinburgh fishwife from Kay's 'Original Portraits' 1792. She wears a spotted muslin headscarf and boldly striped skirts. Her basket is full of oysters for selling in the streets or at houses.

Ministers noticed a great difference in costume, also, when people came to the kirk in their best clothes. The Cambuslang Minister wrote:

> When a farmer's family went to the kirk (in 1750) he and his sons wore suits of home-made cloth, plaidin hose and blue or black bonnets; his wife and daughters were dressed in gowns of their own spinning, both cloaks and hoods, worsted stockings and leather shoes.

By 1790 things had changed:

> He and his sons wore suits of English cloth, worsted or cotton stockings and hats; his wife and daughters were dressed in printed calico or silk gowns, scarlet wool or silk cloaks, silk bonnets, white thread stockings and cloth shoes.

Other writers, including Robert Burns (1759–94), tell us of the finery worn by young ploughmen and farmers, plush or corduroy breeches, long broadcloth coats, velvet waistcoats, fine linen shirts with ruffled fronts, fringed muslin cravats and black silk shoulder knots. Women wore gay muslins, silks and printed cottons.

These descriptions show that many country people were better-off and that there were new goods to buy, textiles

This view of a cottage interior, by David Allan, says a great deal about cooking, costume, customs and manners, furnishings and toys. Allan drew many scenes of social life.

made in mills in Scotland as well as in England.

The people who wore this finery still lived in the roughest houses. Good building materials (dressed stone, seasoned timber, laths, planking, slates and plaster) were too expensive and too difficult to transport.

In some parts, such as East Lothian, the soil was richer and the tenant farmers more prosperous and their houses roomier and more comfortable. The house area was about the same, but the barn at one end and the byre and stable at the other were separate buildings with their own entrances.

The farmhouse was divided into two rooms, the but and the ben. The but was the main living room, used as kitchen, dining room, sitting room and bedroom for the grown-up daughters and female servants. The ben was a better room, sometimes with a wooden floor instead of beaten earth, and the farmer, his wife and the young children used it as their sleeping place.

The sons slept upstairs in the garrets, rooms made by laying floorboards across the ceiling joists and lit by little windows cut in the gable-ends. Male farm servants slept on a platform built over the horses' heads in the stable.

Farmhouses like this had chimneys cut into the gables and in the but wooden settles were set in the inglenook to make a cosy place to sit in the evening.

Rural household utensils in the eighteenth century. Top row, left to right: wrought iron toaster, baking stone. Bottom, left to right: bread spade, girdle, bannock spade.

Left to right: bowl, luggie – with two horn spoons.

In these houses the walls were higher, about 2 metres, and plastered, while the small windows were filled with diamond-shaped panes of glass set in lead. Kitchen utensils were different, too. By the end of the century a farmer's wife could buy cast-iron pots, kettles and pails which were cheaper and longer-lasting than those made of copper or wood.

All these houses were luxurious compared with those of the poor cottars. They lived in hovels made of rough stones or turf about 4 metres square, with a smoke-hole in the divot roof and one glass-less window protected by a wooden shutter.

Even as late as 1871 a third of country dwellers reared families of eight or more in single-roomed houses, while about another third never had more than two rooms.

Both in town and country it was hard to get away from dirt and smell. Human and animal manure was piled up in a great heap in the courtyard before the farm-house, and visitors wisely kept to the causeway of flat stones that led up to the house door. If they stepped off they might easily sink up to the knee in foul smelling mud and water.

Countryfolk forgot the hard-working day at the local fair. Dressed in their best, they gaped at the wandering jugglers, acrobats and candy-sellers. Old people gossiped, young people flirted and, according to the ministers, they all took far too much whisky, snuff and tobacco.

Communion time brought crowds of people together from villages and farm-touns to listen to open-air sermons. They found time at these 'Holy Fairs' for merry-making as well.

At Hallowe'en and Hogmanay they still celebrated the old pagan feasts, partly for the fun of it and also because many people still believed in witches and fairies and magic. Burns' poem about a Hallowe'en describes how the young people, half in terror, tried to foresee who their future wives and husbands would be like. One way was to peep into a mirror, and another was to pull up a cabbage stump.

Christenings, funerals and marriages were social occasions, also. The Penny Weddings were cheerful affairs. All the guests contributed food and drink for the feast; in earlier days the gift was a penny.

Bride and groom lead off the dance in David Allan's 'Penny Wedding'. The company below make merry and young spectators look down from the loft. Garrets in a farmhouse were usually built in this style.

Most activities changed slowly over the centuries before the invention of steam-driven machinery. This picture of Glasgow Fair was drawn in 1825. It includes the same kinds of entertainment as those of the Middle Ages – though costume has changed.

David Allan's 'Highland Dance' shows dancing in the open air to the music of strings and bagpipes. The highland costume is already changing from that shown on page 73.

The inn scene at the beginning of 'Tam o'Shanter', the famous poem by Robert Burns. Tam sits drinking in the inglenook by a blazing fire with the landlord and landlady and his crony Souter Johnny. When he leaves the inn, full of drink, Tam is chased by witches and warlocks whom he disturbs in Alloway Kirk.

Men gathered at country inns, such as the famous inn where Tam o'Shanter tarried too long and nearly got carried off by the devil.

Women had their own special gatherings, the 'Rockings'. Every little farmhouse made its own yarn for weaving and unmarried girls spent so much time spinning that the name 'spinster' is still used today.

Spinning took up all the spare minutes between farm and household tasks, as well as evening hours. Often the girls took their distaffs and spindles to a barn or cottage and did their spinning in company, gossiping and 'spinning yarns'. These meetings were known as 'rockings' after the 'rocks' or spindles used by the women.

Sometimes the young men came along, too, and there would be dancing, and so the distaffs and spindles, or 'rocks' and 'reels' gave their names to Scottish dances.

Rev. Robert Walker by Henry Raeburn of Edinburgh. Skating was a traditional sport.

A girl spinning with distaff and spindle (p. 56).

A cartoon picture of David Dale.

When the linen industry and then the cotton industry became important in Scotland manufacturers found plenty of skilled spinners and weavers who could handle the new fine yarns.

Many Scottish merchants hoped to sell great supplies of linen in England after the Union but they had no success. Scottish flax was poor and the finished linen was coarse and yellow. Most trade and industry in Scotland did badly and the Parliament at Westminster set up a special Board of Commissioners to find ways of helping them. The Board spent its money wisely, giving money to flax growers, bringing in expert spinners and weavers from Flanders and France, and setting up Spinning Schools where more girls could learn to use spinning wheels.

After 1727 the linen trade began to flourish, especially in Forfar and Fife, which specialised in making coarser cloths, and in Lanarkshire and Renfrewshire, which concentrated on the finer

The type of handloom used before power-driven looms made factory-produced cloth cheaper.

cloth needed for handkerchiefs, neckerchiefs and dress materials. Linen goods were printed in gay stripes and checks and the brightly striped headscarves popular with women became known as 'Glasgows'.

Linen merchants often became rich. The most famous was David Dale, who served his time as a weaver in Paisley and then opened a shop in Glasgow High Street in 1761.

View of Glasgow 1764 by Robert Paul. The tower of the Merchants' House (see page 95) is second from the right. Towers from left to right: Hutcheson's Hospital – then in Argyle Street (see Heriot's School on page 87), Old Ramshorn Church, Glasgow Cathedral, University (the Old College), Tron Church, the Tolbooth, Merchants' House and St. Andrews Church.

His business was very successful. He imported fine yarn from Flanders and had it woven by local weavers. By 1794 he was interested in the idea of using cotton instead of linen. Cotton cloth was cheaper, softer and finer. One manufacturer, James Menteith, set up a whole village of cotton weavers in Anderston, a village which then lay just outside Glasgow.

Helped by Richard Arkwright, inventor of the Water Frame, Dale chose a site for his mill by the Falls of Clyde near Lanark. Here the fast-flowing water was harnessed to drive spinning machines.

Work in the cotton mills called for quick fingers rather than great strength. Women and children made the best workers, for they were biddable and cheap to employ.

The mills were huge by eighteenth-century standards. In 1795 Dale employed 1334 workers. He had to provide homes for these workpeople. He built long rows of tenements in the narrow valley by the mills, and called his settlement New Lanark.

Dale was a very religious man and highly interested in education, so the apprentices attended school from 7.30 to 9 p.m. The school also catered for the children of the village so that 570 children attended the school, which was taught by sixteen teachers. It was open on Sundays for those who could not squeeze into the kirk and for religious education in the afternoon. There was no work on Sundays.

Among those employed were 398 orphan children taken from the poor houses of Edinburgh and Glasgow. Dale got good value from these 'apprentices' who received no wages but were kept, clothed and fed until the age of fifteen.

Visitors thought he treated his child workers very well. The working day lasted $11\frac{1}{2}$ hours, from 6 a.m. to 7 p.m. with half an hour off for breakfast at nine and an hour's break for dinner at two.

Food was plentiful. The children could eat as much bread as they wanted before starting work, and for breakfast and supper they had porridge and milk. For dinner they ate broth with potatoes and bread, with meat one day and cheese on the next.

EIGHTEENTH CENTURY: Cotton

Above : Corra Linn in 1812. The Falls of Clyde have today lost much of their splendour through being harnessed for hydro-electric power, except when the sluices are opened.   Below : David Dale's model village of New Lanark is crammed into the narrow steep-sided valley of the Clyde. The mills no longer work but the rows of houses have been renovated into modern flats.

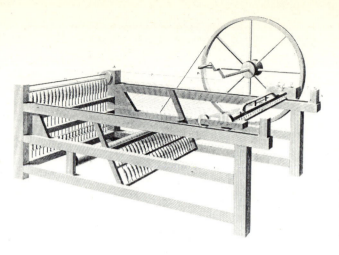

A hand-spinner, using a spinning wheel, could spin thread on to one spool at a time. Using the Spinning Jenny (invented by James Hargreaves in 1765) the spinner could feed thread on to as many as 100 spindles at once.

A lowland foot soldier of the regiment later called the King's Own Scottish Borderers. The unusual plant in the foreground records the regiment's service in Minorca 1769–1775.

The factory children wore cotton clothes in summer and linen dresses or woollen suits in the winter. As was common in eighteenth-century Scotland they went barefoot in the summer months.

At night they slept in six large dormitories, three to a bed, with proper sheets and blankets. Dale paid a great deal of attention to health and hygiene. Dormitories were scrubbed every week and whitewashed once a year. The children's clothes were washed every fortnight.

When they reached the age of fifteen the apprentices were dismissed since they would now have to be paid. Girls usually went into domestic service and became maidservants in the houses of the gentry. Boys joined the army, became apprentice joiners, carpenters or, very often, weavers.

Dale and other manufacturers built big water-driven mills at Catrine, Blantyre, Dean, Balfron, Stanley and other places but most weaving still had to be done on hand looms until the 1820s; there was a great deal of home spinning, too. By 1800 there were 82 000 people working in the cotton industry, in mills, at home or as part-time workers.

One of the most unusual and remarkable men to come from the farming and weaving villages of west Scotland was Robert Burns whose poems were published in Kilmarnock in 1786. They stunned the literary clubs in Edinburgh who found it hard to believe that an Ayrshire farmer would have anything to write or even be able to write it.

Burns really owed little to the parish school, for he lived too far away. His father, a devout and religious man, persuaded his neighbours to join in paying a young student named John Murdoch to come and teach grammar, writing, arithmetic and psalm-singing to their children. Murdoch was paid sixpence a day and taught them for two years, till Burns was nine and had to start full-time work on the farm.

Before his poems appeared in print, Robert Burns had decided to emigrate. His father had died of overwork and disappointment as one farm after another failed to give him a decent living. Now Burns found himself a successful poet,

Portrait of Robert Burns by Alexander Nasmyth. Both believed that people are of equal worth, regardless of wealth or rank. So Nasmyth could get no more portrait work from the rich.

invited to the fashionable city of Edinburgh to meet the cream of Scottish society.

A shoemaker at work drawn by C. Smith about 1810.

David Allan's 'Fireman' does not seem well equipped to deal with the fire.

Edinburgh chimney sweeps : ladder, brush and sack.

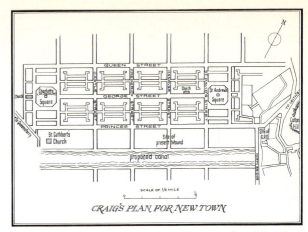

CRAIG'S PLAN FOR NEW TOWN

Edinburgh New Town was built to Craig's plan but the proposal for a canal was abandoned. The modern aerial view is from the west.

21 Eighteenth Century: CITY LIFE

Eighteenth-century Edinburgh attracted people from all parts of Scotland, ministers to the General Assembly, wealthy merchants to the Convention of Royal Burghs and nobles and country gentlemen to their town houses.

Above all, Edinburgh was the place where the chief Law Court met, the Court of Session. Many Edinburgh lawyers became wealthy men and bought up country estates.

As the Old Town became more crowded richer people began to look for more elegant and spacious houses out of the smell and stir of the packed closes and narrow streets. The Lord Provost, George Drummond, found the answer: he planned a New Town to be built on re-claimed swamp land by the Nor' Loch. The Town Council invited architects to enter a competition to find the best plan and in 1762 it was won by a 27-year-old architect named James Craig.

He suggested a grid-iron pattern. Three long wide thoroughfares, George Street, Queen Street and Princes Street were linked by cross streets and at each end of George Street there was a handsome square. Many of the elegant houses were designed by the great Scots architect Robert Adam.

With the development of the New Town, Edinburgh flourished as a centre of arts and fashion.

It had the first licensed theatre in Scotland, opened in 1762 in spite of the disapproval of the Kirk.

Another fashionable meeting-place was the Assembly Rooms, where ladies and gentlemen gathered to dance stately minuets and quadrilles. The dances were very formal affairs, the ladies in hooped skirts of velvet or silk, their hair piled high over wire cages, powdered and decorated, and the gentlemen in wigs, long tight-waisted coats, embroidered

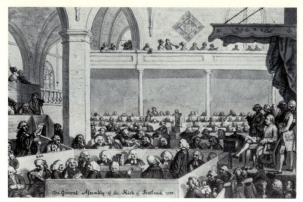

Bewigged ministers and other gentlemen listen to a discussion in the General Assembly of the Kirk, the only national assembly in Scotland since 1707.

A view of Edinburgh in 1817, showing the 'Mound', built on rubbish piled in the middle of the Nor' Loch to link Princes Street with the High Street. Gardens now fill the hollow.

This Leith oyster cellar, depicted by Burnett, does not look as if it were meant for high society.

The ladies' hairstyles and dresses of 1800 were better for dancing than earlier fashions.

'The Painter's Wife' by Allan Ramsay, son of the Edinburgh poet and bookseller. The painter, born in 1713, was a highly educated and cultured man. He had studied in Rome and spoke several languages.

waistcoats, tight breeches and swords.

If they wanted more lively dancing they could join the merrier set who gathered in the oyster cellars to drink portar, eat oysters and dance Scottish reels.

Music lovers could attend performances of Handel and Mozart at the meetings of the Musical Society at St. Cecilia's Hall. Those interested in literature joined Scotland's first lending library, in Allan Ramsay's shop near the Mercat Cross. Here they met people with similar tastes and, after the fashion of the day, they formed clubs and societies.

This view from the south side of the Clyde in Glasgow. The bridge is the Broomielaw (Jamaica Street bridge) built 1763–1768 as Glasgow's second bridge and known as the 'Bonnie Brig' because of the decorative circles above each pier. The costume indicates that the drawing was made about 1800. The bridge was rebuilt 1832–1835. The smoking conical building on the left is the glassworks.

A wooden tobacco sign in the form of a Red Indian. By 1740 Glasgow merchants handled over half the American tobacco crop through their warehouses – most of it being exported to France. This and other forms of trade made Glasgow the chief shipping and commercial town of Scotland.

While Edinburgh thrived as the centre of fashion and high culture, Glasgow became the chief city of business. With the Union came the chance to build up trade with the North American colonies. Its merchants made great fortunes in sugar, rum and tobacco, and controlled most of the supply of tobacco to Europe. The American planters had to send all their tobacco to Britain first.

The tobacco trade slumped after the American War of Independence when planters could sell direct to other European countries. The cotton trade took its place. The Clyde was deepened so that ocean-going ships could come right up to the Broomielaw and in 1790 the city was linked to the east coast by the Forth-Clyde Canal.

In the middle of the century Glasgow was still a small town, with its merchants meeting at the Cross and carrying out their business on the plain stones, but thirty years later they met in the Chamber

Merchants meet by King William's statue in front of their Tontine Hotel (over the arcade) and the Tolbooth (guarded by a sentrybox). The plainstones (the only paving in the city) are fenced off. The Tontine Hotel was used as coffee house, assembly room and club.

A bank note from one of Glasgow's earliest banks, the Ship Bank. Notes were sometimes hard to change as small coins were often scarce.

of Commerce, founded in 1782 by Patrick Colquhoun, Provost of Glasgow.

As in Edinburgh, the wealthier citizens moved out into new suburbs, to George Square or Blythswood, or to the village of Gorbals on the south side of the river. Their old flats and tenements quickly filled up with people who flocked to work in Glasgow. The city's population shot up to 83 700 in 1801.

Glasgow could not match Edinburgh as a social centre, but its old university had some remarkable and world-famous professors, including Adam Smith and John Anderson. Smith was an economist whose book *The Wealth of Nations* was widely read by statesmen and businessmen. John Anderson is famous as the scientist who encouraged the inventor James Watt and began evening classes for adults at the Andersonian Institute. This was the first technical college in Europe and eventually became (1966) the University of Strathclyde.

Glasgow merchants were well-educated men, interested in literature and the arts, and they formed clubs on the Edinburgh pattern.

An open-air exhibition of paintings in the courtyard of the old Glasgow University in 1761.

A country inn yard showing passengers mounting a very clumsy-looking windowless coach with enormous wheels. Two men sprawl on the roof top and an old woman sits in the basket used for luggage. Later coaches had rails for the outside passengers to hang on to, and the basket gave way to a boot.

22 THE TRANSPORT REVOLUTION

The old trackways could not stand up to the needs of eighteenth-century merchants and travellers. Wheels sank deep into the mud and axles shattered as the vehicles bounced among ruts and stones.

Even Wade's gravel-surfaced roads could not stand up to wheeled traffic. When Lord Lovat drove from Inverness to Edinburgh in 1740 he took eleven days. The coach's rear axle broke twice and the front axle once. At times he got squads of men to drag the coach to the nearest black-smith while his daughters perched unhappily behind the postilions on saddle-less horses.

Waggoners tried to carry heavy goods by fitting enormous broad-rimmed wheels and harnessing large teams of horses.

Wealthy passengers could hire a post-chaise and do the journey to London in six days, with luck.

Turnpike Roads were built by local landowners who clubbed together to lay new roads. They got their money back by

Thomas Telford, the great engineer, built fishing ports, canals and highways (including 1200 bridges) in all parts of the country.

making travellers pay tolls every few miles along the road. The names Toll-cross, Allander Toll, and dozens of similar names tell us where these toll gates used to be.

Improved roads meant faster traffic. In 1766 a fast 'Fly' coach carried four passengers between Edinburgh and Glasgow in nine hours. Soon there were regular stage coach services between Edinburgh and the towns of Glasgow, Stirling and Perth.

The wheels of a two-ton coach travelling at 13 km/h tore up the road surfaces very quickly but John Loudon Macadam, an Ayrshire landowner, solved the problem when he laid his first new road between Ayr and Maybole in 1787.

The road was dug out to a depth of about 30 cm and filled with very small stones which became packed tight under the wheels of carts and carriages. Modern 'tar macadam' roads use this idea though the stones are now bound with tar to give a firmer surface.

Coach travel was a painful business. Inside passengers were terribly cramped on the narrow seats with knees nearly touching those of the person opposite. The outside passengers, perched more than 3 metres above the ground, had only a narrow rail to cling to. Whole coaches were sometimes buried in deep drifts on places like Fenwick Moor.

The postilion pays the toll-keeper his fee for letting a post chaise pass. The passenger inside looks rather nervous; perhaps she is worried about the luggage balanced on the roof. Averaging 18 km/h, a fast chaise could bring important news from London in 33 hours.

Ostlers steady the lively horses as the Glasgow mail coach prepares to leave the 'Bull and Mouth' inn, London, while a spectator looks down from one of the galleries that connect the upper rooms.

In 1784 the Post Office began a mail coach service covering the whole of Britain.

Mail coaches carried only a few passengers, some inside and some out, as well as driver and guard. The stage coaches run by private companies carried as many as 15 passengers.

Smartly painted, upper panels a glossy black, lower panels a deep maroon with gilded coats-of-arms, and wheels post-office red, the mail coaches brought a new idea of regularity and punctuality into eighteenth century life.

Operating the mails was big business and the Post Office insisted on perfect time-keeping. The guard's most important

equipment, apart from his blunderbuss, horse pistols and horn, was his sealed watch, carried in a padlocked glass fronted box. Postmasters checked the mail coaches' time at each stop.

By 1830 the speed of the mail coaches was set at 16 km/h. It was a killing pace for horses. They had to be changed every 16 km. There were 40 stages on the Edinburgh–London run and to keep mail and stage coaches operating, thousands of horses were needed.

The speed and safety of the mail was the main consideration. When the mail coach stuck in heavy snow drifts by the Devil's Beef Tub near Moffat, driver and guard tried to ride the horses through on their

The old 'Saracen's Head', built in the Gallow-gate, Glasgow in 1754, with stones taken from the old Bishop's Castle, was the chief coaching station for many years, with stables for sixty horses. The first London–Glasgow mail coach reached it on 7 July 1788.

The guard carried a special watch, in a padlocked brass case in a pouch suspended from his shoulder. The postmaster used it to write in the time of the coach's departure. He also entered the time according to the local clocks or even sundials.

A sleepy gatekeeper at Stamford Hill turnpike lets the Edinburgh mail coach through on the last moonlit stage of the journey to London. The journey had been cut from seventy-eight hours in 1784 to forty-two in 1820.

A stage coach 'The Bruce' passes two other coaches stuck in snowdrifts in the 1830s. Outside passengers need their triple-caped coats.

own. Then they struggled through the blizzard on foot until they died of exposure, leaving the precious mail firmly fastened to a stout post.

The arrival of the mail was enormously exciting. Glasgow businessmen waited at their special clubroom, the Tontine Coffee House, for the blare of the guard's horn and the blunderbuss shot which announced the mail was ready.

When the mail coach brought news of a great victory such as Trafalgar (1805) the horses were wreathed in laurels, the guard wore his best gold-laced hat and scarlet coat and a red flag fluttered from the coach roof.

Glasgow businessmen waited eagerly for the mail and the newspapers. When the papers came there was a wild scramble as the waiter, Charles Gordon, threw the whole lot up into the air. Dignified lawyers and insurance men joined in this game with gusto until the day one gentleman had his teeth knocked out.

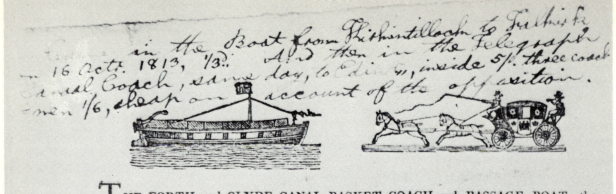

THE FORTH and CLYDE CANAL BASKET COACH and PASSAGE BOAT, the Cheapest, Safest, and most Comfortable Travelling of any Conveyance between Edinburgh and Glasgow.

This 1813 handbill advertises a new means of travelling between Glasgow and Edinburgh, and a passenger records his journey by boat and 'Telegraph'. Coaches often carried names to advertise their speed: 'Express', 'Tallyho', 'New Times'.

A fishing boat passes through one of the locks on the Caledonian Canal. Telford's great canal never became an important waterway. Fishing and tourist boats are the main traffic.

When bulk transport was needed to shift heavy loads of coal, ore and manufactured goods the Scots followed the English example of cutting canals. The Monkland Canal to link Lanarkshire mines with Glasgow and the Forth–Clyde Canal linking east and west were completed in 1790.

Other canals were built later, the Crinan Canal in 1801, the Inverurie–Aberdeen Canal in 1807, the Union Canal between Edinburgh and Falkirk and the huge Caledonian Canal in 1822.

Linked with stage coach services the canals provided a wonderfully fast service for passengers. The fastest and smoothest ride was on the Glasgow–Paisley Canal, where William Houston harnessed coach horses to a special barge. The light iron hull was 21·2 metres long, 1·7 metres wide and drew only 40 cm of water. It could hold 90 passengers and two fast horses, frequently changed, pulled it along at 19 km/h. Twelve boats operated daily between Glasgow and Paisley, carrying 423 186 passengers in 1836.

Excited crowds watched the opening of the Glasgow–Garnkirk railway on 27 September 1831. Most of the passengers were in open trucks and were astounded at the speed (about 7½ mph).

In 1802 the first successful steamboat, the Charlotte Dundas, was used to pull barges across country from the Forth to Port Dundas.

The coming of steam put both coaches and canals out of business. The first steam trains ran on the Glasgow–Garnkirk and the Edinburgh–Dalkeith lines in 1831, and the Dundee–Newtyle line in 1832. After 1840 railway lines began to link the lowland towns and penetrate northwards, from Edinburgh to Perth and Dundee in 1847 and Inverness in 1863.

Railways joined England and Scotland more closely together. The Edinburgh–Berwick line was completed in 1846 and the Glasgow–Carlisle line in 1848.

The effects of rail transport were soon felt by all classes of people all over the country for, by law, the railway companies had to provide cheap transport and passengers could travel first, second or third class. Mail was speeded up (the 'penny post' came in 1840) and businessmen, workers and tourists travelled in comfort.

William Symington's 'stern-wheeler', the 'Charlotte Dundas', proved the value of steam when it towed two laden sloops 19 miles in six hours against strong head winds, on the Forth–Clyde canal in 1802.

Watt's double-acting rotative steam engine. James Watt of Greenock (1736–1819) improved

the older atmospheric engine by fitting a condenser. He also adapted the engine to drive machinery. Steam power gradually replaced wind, water and muscle power in industry. For his own use, Watt designed this little stove with three covers to fit the top: a lid with chimney (while fire is drawing), a kettle and a lidded pan.

A nineteenth-century steam engine used to drive a threshing machine, one of the first steps in replacing human and animal muscle power on the farm.

The railways affected life in the country, too. Already landlords had realised that they could make great profits by supplying towns with food and they now rented out their land to farmers who could pay the highest rents. The new farms were solid blocks of land rented to one man and so the old farm-towns and separate rigs vanished.

The farmers soon made use of new Scottish inventions, James Small's swing-plough, Patrick Bell's reaper and Andrew Meikle's threshing machine. Farmers in the Lothians were the first to harness steam engines to drive the threshers. Unwanted farm labourers drifted into the towns.

Scientific farming methods made farmers well-to-do. They could now afford to build roomy stone houses, with three rooms downstairs and three or more upstairs. They furnished them better than the gentry had done in the eighteenth century, with mahogany furniture, carpets and even pianos. Scots farming became famous for efficiency.

New industries and transport services brought new kinds of work for ordinary people. Much of it was hard and monotonous and in the industrial areas working and living conditions were dangerously unhealthy. Neither Parliament nor the Town Councils realised how great the changes were.

Scotland had its first great ironworks at Carron, begun in 1769 and especially famous for its naval guns. Now the centre of iron manufacture swung over to Airdrie, Coatbridge and Motherwell after David Mushett found deposits of Blackband Ironstone in Lanarkshire in 1801.

This mixture of coal and iron was not easy to smelt until John Neilson suggested that hot air should be blasted into the furnaces instead of cold. The method was so successful that Scotland became the world's second largest iron producer, next in size to England.

The need for coal and iron expanded rapidly with the use of steam engines for all sorts of purposes. James Watt had adapted his engine to drive mill machinery in 1781, William Symington used it in a steam boat in 1788 and William Murdoch invented a steam locomotive in 1784.

Adam Smith explained that a nation's wealth was its people, working at producing goods for sale. Manufacturers could create a rich nation by using their profits to make more goods and to provide more jobs.

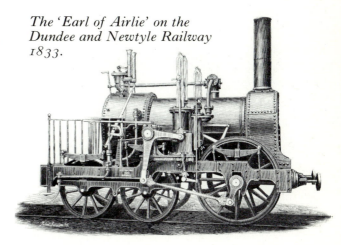

The 'Earl of Airlie' on the Dundee and Newtyle Railway 1833.

Two pictures from the report of the Royal Commission on the Mines 1842.   Left: a girl carrying coal (Janet Cumming, 11 years old: I carry the large bits of coal from wall-face to pit bottom ... the weight is usually a hundred-weight.)   Right: children being drawn up the mine shaft. There is no cage so they hang on as well as they can to the winding rope.

Coal mining had begun in the twelfth century. Until 1799 miners were little better than serfs. They often pledged that their children would serve in the mine all their lives, in return for an *arles*, a gift made by the mine owner at the time of the christening.

Sometimes criminals had been handed over as slaves, like Alexander Stewart, convicted of theft in Perth in 1701. He was sentenced to death, for there were over two hundred crimes for which people could be hanged in those days. Instead, he was granted to Sir John Erskine of Alva, to work as Sir John's 'perpetual servant'.

Miners worked under horrible conditions, even though they were free in the nineteenth century. They usually worked in family teams. Men hewed the coal, helped by the older boys who, according to age and strength, were known as 'quarter men' at 10 and 'three-quarter men' at 16 or 17.

The deep mines of the west began to use winding gear to lift coal to the surface. In Fife and the Lothians pits were shallow and women and girls carried coal to the surface on their backs in large creels.

Little Margaret Leveston could carry 25 kg when she was six, and another girl, Jane Johnston, carried 100 kg when she was fifteen.

Children like Rebecca Sim, aged 11, were harnessed to coal waggons with ropes and chains. Her task, with her sister, was

Alexander Stewart's collar.

David Allan's 1780 picture of a shed at Lead-hills, Lanarkshire, where boys break lumps of lead ore for smelting in a furnace. Lead miners ceased to be serfs sooner than coal miners — largely because skilled workers had to be attracted from a distance for the processing. In 1780 most industry was on a small scale. Large concerns included Leadhills, the Carron Iron-works and some coal mines.

to pull a waggon weighing 350 kg. Big brother George, aged 14, helped them 'up the brae'.

Women and children were banned from mines in 1842. Janet Cumming, 11, described at an enquiry how she had been a coal bearer for two years, collecting the coal and carrying a 50 kg creel. The roof was so low that she had to bend both back and knees to pass along, and often the water in the tunnel came above her calves. She worked from 5 a.m. to 5 p.m. but on Fridays she worked all night till Saturday noon.

George Reid, aged 16, had hewn coal since he was 10. He found it 'horrible sore work' wielding a pick in a seam 66 cm high. The 9-year-old boys employed at Carron worked in front of the scorching furnaces, often burned by sparks and hot metal and found life in the ironworks just as bad.

Coalface in 1910.

Modern shearer loader at the coalface.

One of the few handloom weavers still working in the nineteenth century at Kirriemuir. His equipment looks traditional and well used.

The main room of the weaver's cottage at Kilbarchan, Renfrewshire, with the bed recess found in many Scottish homes.

A holiday outing for the more prosperous workers in the 1830s. They head for the countryside in a variety of conveyances.

Eighteenth-century handweavers had been the best paid workers in Scotland, working only four days a week and owning their own houses. They dressed like the upper classes in long gilt-buttoned coats, ruffled shirts, smart knee breeches and powdered wigs. Life for thousands of them became grim as farm workers made redundant by new farm machinery, dispossessed highlanders and Irish immigrants came in search of work. Weavers were now so badly paid that they had to move into slum quarters and dress in rags.

The best paid textile workers now were the male cotton spinners who had the strength and skill needed to handle heavy machinery.

In the 1820s they began to earn good wages, enough to rent a decent room and kitchen house and to fill it with mahogany furniture: a proper bedstead, table and chairs, chest of drawers, china cupboard and book-shelf. A prize possession was a grandfather clock. Their families ate well, with fresh meat for dinner and luxuries such as tea, coffee, sugar and white bread.

The cotton spinners kept wages high by forming unions. They knew employers would cut their wages if there were more spinners than jobs. There were often bitter riots as they used violence to stop non-union men entering the trade.

They had seen what happened to the handweavers when too many newcomers came into the industry.

Conditions were specially bad for the women and children in the smaller mills. In James Kirkland's mills at Dunfermline the linen was kept damp so that it would not snap. His workers, girls between 10 and 14, worked a 12 hour day

Pulleys and driving belts feed power to the looms in a weaving mill in 1843. By this time the Factory Acts had banned the employment of children under 13 and appointed inspectors to see that the regulations were carried out.

standing barefooted on a wet, dirty flagged floor, their clothes soaking wet, continuously sprayed by the water thrown off from the machines.

Mill hours were long and employers sometimes cheated by altering the clocks to suit themselves. Even in good mills the continual standing gave workers varicose veins and children working in a temperature of over 24°C suffered dreadful accidents. Cogs and pulleys did enormous damage when ragged clothes, fingers, arms and hair got tangled in the machinery.

It was better in the bigger mills at New Lanark, Catrine, Deanston or Stanley in Perthshire. Here the employers kept the mills clean, built houses, churches and schools. In New Lanark, Robert Owen, David Dale's son-in-law, encouraged adult education, organised the workers to clean their houses of bugs, lice and fleas and opened a co-operative shop in the village.

Robert Owen (1771–1858) believed that good conditions would make people good. He wanted people to co-operate. He was ahead of his time but his ideas inspired co-operative societies, trade unions and socialist communities.

Owen's New Lanark school for children of 2–10 years was a pattern for the future.

Canal diggers were known as 'navigators'. Later, other construction workers were called 'navvies'.

24 Nineteenth Century: INDUSTRIAL WORKERS

More people moved into the coal fields and industrial towns all through the nineteenth century. They came from the highlands and islands, from overcrowded lowland farms and above all they came from Ireland.

Steamboats made the crossing easy when the Belfast–Portpatrick services opened in 1818. By 1841 over 125 000 Irish immigrants had settled in Scotland, mostly in the west. An even bigger flow came in 1845 and 1846 when the potato crop failed and brought starvation to Ireland. Thousands of Irish died, over a million and a quarter sailed to America and about 115 000 came to Scotland. In 1851 Irish-born people made up 15 % of the population of the west of Scotland, and 18 % of the people of Glasgow.

Many found jobs as 'navvies' on the new railways which began to cover the country in the 1840s, linking all the outlying parts of Britain together as never before. Others swelled the population of the lowlands, which grew from 1 608 420 in 1801 to 2 888 742 in 1851 and 4 472 103 in 1901. The people who came to the mining villages and cities found little comfort, bad housing and few amenities.

In mining villages the colliery owners built long rows of 2-roomed houses, without sanitation or water supply. The houses soon became horribly over-

Tall closely built Glasgow tenements in 1868 blocked out daylight and clean air.

High School Wynd, Edinburgh, in 1837, one narrow overcrowded street of the 'Old Town'.

crowded, for many of the incomers were single men and as many as fourteen might lodge with a family who rented a colliery house.

Mining villages were rough places, without schools or churches and the only shop belonged to the mine-owner, who often sold on credit at high prices and made large profits from the sale of cheap whisky. At the same time the windswept mining villages were often healthier than the crowded cities.

Town workers ran greater health risks than their ancestors though their one-roomed tenement houses were no more crowded than country cottages and were probably warmer, drier and less smoky. City dirt and poor food shortened the lives of many. Doctors soon noticed that

By contrast, mid-twentieth-century houses at Cumber-nauld New Town, famous for its open layout and the skilful use of trees.

fever epidemics hit hardest at the poor. Upper-class Edinburgh citizens in the early nineteenth century lived on average 47 years, but labourers only 26 years.

Moray Place, Edinburgh, from an engraving of 1831. In the New Town, wealthy people were able to live in spacious houses well laid out in streets, squares and crescents pleasing to the eye – with gardens to make them more so.

Libberton Wynd, Edinburgh, in 1854. Seventy years before, Robert Burns met his friends in Dowie's Tavern, here renamed after the poet.

All the big cities had their slum districts but Glasgow and Edinburgh had the worst. In Glasgow the tenements were built so close together that many rooms never got any direct sunlight. Filthy closes led to foul stairs, dirty corridors and one-roomed houses, divided up by box beds and sometimes holding more than one family.

Sanitation was non-existent. People in the upper houses poured away their liquid waste into a tank outside the stair window. The wooden drain pipe was not connected to drain or sewer, however, and its contents simply splashed on to the back court.

In Edinburgh the great gulf between rich and poor was shown in the Old and New Towns. A wealthy lawyer in 1830 had his own four-storeyed house, with servants' quarters in the basement and

This cartoon shows a lecturer demonstrating a scientific experiment at the Andersonian Institute, Glasgow, in the 1820s. Parish schools had always catered for girls as well as boys and it is interesting to see a number of women in the class.

Shuttle Row, now a memorial to Livingstone. A table in an upstairs one-room house was his study until, at 23, he moved to Glasgow.

dining room, drawing room, library, nursery and bedrooms arranged on the upper floors. One Old Town tenement in the 1860s, the Middle Meal-Market Stair, had five floors also, each with 11 or 12 rooms and contained 56 families, a total of 248 people. There was no tap, sink or toilet in the whole building.

Crowded living conditions did not stop determined people working for a better life. The industrial age brought new ideas and opportunities to many.

David Livingstone, for example, was born in a one-roomed house in Shuttle Street, Blantyre, in a tenement near James Menteith's cotton mill. The house was one of twenty-four opening off from a spiral staircase.

His father made his living selling tea from door to door. A religious man, a Sunday School teacher, he was too poor to keep David at school after the age of ten, and David went to work in the mill. He was a strong boy and stood up well to the long hours, 6 a.m. to 8 p.m. and at night he attended school for two hours. By day he kept his Latin book propped up on the machine as he worked.

By the age of 23 he had saved enough money for a 2-year course at the Andersonian Institute, Glasgow. Here, and in London with help from a missionary society, he qualified as a medical missionary and by the age of 28, in 1841, he was ready to set out for Africa to begin his work as missionary and explorer.

Henry Bell's 'Comet', launched in 1812 at Helensburgh, was the first really successful steamship. She plied between Glasgow, Oban, Fort William and Mull – using sails, too.

An 1820 painting of the steamship 'Majestic', built at Greenock to carry mails and passengers between Greenock and Liverpool via Portpatrick and Douglas (IoM) in 24 hours.

The 'Cutty Sark' was built at Dumbarton 1869, last of the fast sailing ships (capable of $17\frac{1}{2}$ knots) that raced to bring the new season's tea from China. Now on view in London.

The 'Servia', first steel vessel of the Cunard Line, built in the 1870s. Clyde shipbuilding companies produced their own steel and by 1900 one quarter of the world's steamships.

25 Late Nineteenth Century: WORK & HOME

The inventions and discoveries of the nineteenth century completely changed the way Scottish people earned their living. By the end of Queen Victoria's reign, in 1901, nearly 500 000 workers depended on the heavy industries (mining, iron and steel manufacture, shipbuilding and engineering) compared with only 200 000 in farming, 28 000 in fishing and 16 000 in the textile trade.

Fishing was still important. There were new ports at Ullapool, Tobermory, Wick and Helmsdale. The use of steam helped fishermen, too: steam trawlers began to sail from Aberdeen in 1882 in search of white fish – cod, ling and haddock. In 1898 steam drifters joined the herring fleets operating from Wick, Aberdeen, Fraserburgh and Peterhead.

Industries boomed right through the century, though the pattern of work changed in the 1860s as the cotton trade died out, except in Lanarkshire and Renfrewshire. Shipbuilding and engineering replaced the cotton industries. Whole towns of shipyard workers grew up: Clydebank did not exist in 1861 but had over 30 000 inhabitants within forty years.

The highlands did not share in the

Herring gutters at Wick in 1905. Fishermen's wives and daughters often moved from port to port, as the fishing boats sailed after the shoals of herring. Their job was to gut and clean the fish.

industrial prosperity of the lowlands. The drift from the north and west continued, in spite of Telford's roads and the work of the Highland and Agricultural Society and the British Fishing Society, both founded at the end of the eighteenth century. There were few clansmen left now, as the government found out when it looked for highland recruits at the time of the Crimean War.

Life for the poor people of Victorian Britain was always overshadowed by the fear of unemployment, sickness and old age. A man who lost his job or could not work had to beg for his living or go into a workhouse. People dreaded old age because it meant living as a burden on their children or a half-starved and comfortless life in an institution.

Indeed, life in the late nineteenth century was an endless struggle. When the people of any town or district all worked at the same occupations, a whole community was badly hit by a firm closing

down or by a local disaster. This was very true of the mining districts.

The anxious crowd at the Blantyre coalmine after the explosion of 1877. 207 men were killed – the worst mining disaster ever in Scotland.

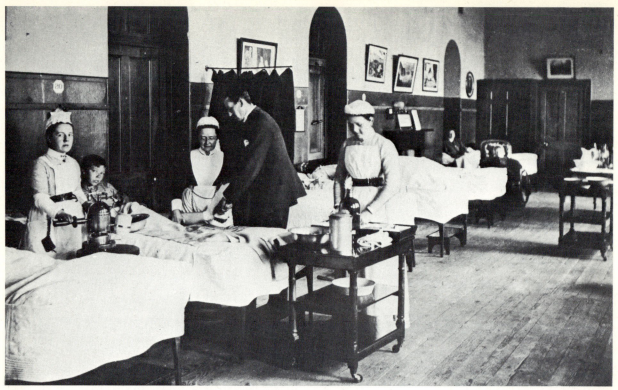

A surgical ward in Aberdeen, 1889. Florence Nightingale's example during the Crimean War had made nursing a well-disciplined and hard-working profession.

James Simpson (1811–1870) began the use of chloroform as an anaesthetic. Surgeons were now able to operate with greater care and undertake more difficult operations.

Joseph Lister, while professor of surgery in Scotland 1860–1877 realised that infection from surgeon's knives and clothes killed many patients. As the first antiseptic he used carbolic acid.

Many women went to work. Worst-off were those who worked in 'sweat-shops', for example, sewing and stitching for clothing manufacturers. Work conditions were foul and wages pitiful, but there were no unions for women, no laws to protect them, and money was needed at home.

Girls went into 'domestic service', as maidservants in middle and upper class homes. In Victorian times, people felt a great gulf lay between those who worked with their hands and those who did not. Everyone who could possibly afford to do so had one or more servants.

Other girls and women found work in offices, for the invention of telephones and typewriters provided new kinds of

Servants' bells at Traquair House. The wealthy employed 'armies' of servants: house staff – butlers, footmen, cooks, maids; personal staff – valets, nurses, governesses; outdoors – gardeners, coachmen, stablemen, gamekeepers.

work very suitable for quick-thinking and quick-fingered girls. Shop girls were needed, too, for the growing number of larger shops that sprang up in the '70s and '80s.

There was work in the new 'services': hospitals wanted nurses and Board Schools needed teachers of all sorts.

The worst social problem was housing, for builders went on with tenement blocks full of 'single-end' and 'room and kitchen' houses even after their health dangers were clear. They built them solidly in stone, with walls up to a metre thick, so

that many still stand today.

Over half the townsfolk lived in these small houses that opened off common stairs in tenement buildings. The tenements started a pattern of crowded living which Scottish people accepted as normal. Even today, Scotland has more crowded houses than any other part of Britain. In 1911, before councils began to build houses, 62·5 % of Glasgow people lived in one or two-roomed houses. In other industrial towns of the west (Coatbridge, Wishaw, Kilsyth, Clydebank, Airdrie and Motherwell) nearly 80 % of people did so.

Bed recesses built in the walls of kitchens and living rooms made up for the lack of proper bedrooms. They were cosy but diseases like tuberculosis spread rapidly.

In the early part of the century few working-class homes had much furniture. As wages improved people tried to copy middle-class styles as far as they could. The many girls who had been 'in service' knew how their 'betters' lived.

A reconstruction of a working class home (in the Kelvingrove Museum, Glasgow). One room could serve as kitchen, living room, bedroom, nursery and (for people like David Livingstone) as study. Mantelpiece and open shelves are used to display china and metal ornaments.

A reconstruction of a middle class drawing room, with every surface covered with bric-a-brac. The piano, not shown, would also carry a load of china ornaments and framed pictures.

A very upper class dining room at Culzean Castle, home of the Kennedys, earls of Cassilis. The magnificent ceiling is typical of the architect, Robert Adam, who had designed the house for the 10th Earl.

People who could, crammed their homes with furniture, tables with fringed cloths, plant stands, display cabinets, occasional tables littered with framed photographs and ornaments. Women spent hours with feather dusters and polish to keep the whole display in order.

Living in tightly packed tenements was not very healthy but it often led to a great feeling of companionship among neigh-bours. Very often neighbours were rela-tives as well, since different generations (grandparents, parents and children) lived in the same building or the same street.

This companionship was strengthened by the way the men's work was done in shipyards, foundries and mines where they worked in gangs or teams. Men came to rely upon a workmate's skill, strength and experience – and working friendships were carried over into leisure hours.

Working men met in the same public house or at the same street corner, followed the same sporting interests, supported the same football teams and paid their dues to the same branch of the Trade Union.

For women running their own homes and for girls in domestic service there was plenty to do.

Cleaning was a full-time job. Industrial towns were filled with grime and greasy soot from coal fires and factory chimneys. No matter where one lived dust or mud was tramped in from the unpaved streets. Women's long skirts and petticoats soon got dirty so that washing was a heavy task. Drying clothes was another problem; kitchens were often filled with steaming clothes hung on lines.

Cooking called for special skills. Coal fires had to be banked at just the right height for simmering and stewing – and for baking if the housewife was lucky enough to have a kitchen range with an oven.

Shopping took up a great deal of time because there were no frozen foods and few that were packaged or tinned. Women had to shop daily because food kept in the stuffy houses went bad very quickly.

As steamships brought cheap wheat from Canada, bacon from Denmark and meat from Argentina in refrigerated ships, poorer people began to eat meat and bread – welcome additions to porridge, potatoes, herring, broth and the economical Scottish dishes such as haggis and sheep's head.

The most popular shops for poor and

From the advertisement of 1862 : From numerous examples of the Sewing Machine exhibited we select the one that has been best subjected to the influence of Art; it is, indeed, a very handsome piece of drawing room furniture. . . . It is certainly the best of the candidates for public favour . . .

Staff outside a tobacconist's and general shop in Airdrie. The name of the shop and the striped pole above the door suggest that there was a barber's in the back room.

Lipton's first shop in Stobcross Street.

Italian ice cream vendors carried on the old tradition of street trading and the ice cream (cheaper than café ice cream) was called hokey pokey. French onion men toured till recently.

thrifty people were those run by Co-operative Societies. These kept prices low by buying in bulk and paid back their profits in 'dividends'.

The idea of co-operatives, like that of trade unions, had come from the active mind of Robert Owen of New Lanark.

There was also a new type of shop whose success depended on the fast transport which linked Scotland with countries overseas. The new shops were 'multiple stores', chains of grocery shops owned by one firm. They kept prices low by buying direct from farmers in Ireland, Denmark and America.

Lipton's and Cooper's of Glasgow were among the first of these stores. Thomas Lipton's first shop was in Stobcross Street, and within a few years he had shops all over Britain. People were attracted by his use of advertising which included stunts such as the scattering of leaflets from balloons and the parade through the streets of giant cheeses pulled by elephants.

Cooper's was also founded in 1871, by Thomas Bishop. His shops were very advanced and his Sauchiehall Street shop was the first in the country to have electric lighting.

26 Late Nineteenth Century: SOCIAL LEGISLATION

After 1856 each county and burgh had to provide a police force, after the pattern of the large burghs or the metropolitan Peelers or Bobbies set up by Sir Robert Peel in 1829. The frock coat and stove pipe hat are a reminder that British police are not soldiers but civilians.

This view of Glasgow in the 1870s shows that water carts still served some parts of the city before water taps were installed at street corners and inside houses.

By 1830, many intelligent and educated people of all classes realised that the government was not running the country properly. Members of Parliament were men of considerable property or wealth and were elected by others of the same kind. They did not understand the needs of the rest of the people, two-thirds of whom now worked in some kind of industry.

The Reform Act of 1832 gave another half million men the right to elect Members of Parliament. Although they were not poor themselves they soon began to choose Members who understood better what was wrong with living and working conditions in towns and factories.

One of the first important Acts swept away the old Scottish Town Councils, made up of merchants and wealthy guild members. Householders in the 79 burghs now elected the councillors they wanted and the Act gave Councils the right to raise their own local taxes, rates.

They spent the money of paving, lighting, laying sewage pipes, bringing in clean water supplies and setting up police forces on the model of Glasgow (1800) and Edinburgh (1805).

Dreadful outbreaks of cholera in the 1840s made Councils move fast in piping water from mountain lochs. Edinburgh Corporation build reservoirs in the Pentland Hills and in 1851 Glasgow Water Board laid a 42 kilometre pipeline from Loch Katrine.

Glasgow Cross in the 1850s. Robert Frame started the first horse-drawn omnibus service in 1845, between Bridgeton and Anderston. Electric lighting began to replace gas in 1893.

Aberdeen Fire Brigade in 1875, with a (horse-drawn) steam-operated pumping engine (p. 121).

Life in the towns improved a great deal as local authorities worked to provide better amenities and services. The big towns, Glasgow, Edinburgh, Dundee and Aberdeen, led the way in providing clean water supplies, sewage and drainage, parks baths, libraries, museums, wash-houses (which were very popular and well used) and hospitals.

There had been gas lighting in some towns since 1818. Gas supplies were gradually improved to provide more homes with gas, although everyone could not afford to install it.

As towns became bigger it became harder to travel between work and home. Private companies began to run 'omnibus' services in the 1870s. By the end of the century the local corporations took them over as public services. Glasgow electrified its tramway system in 1898, beginning a famous tram service which lasted into the 1960s. The old trams travelled along metal tracks in the middle of the street with space at the sides of the street for other vehicles. Many towns owe their wide streets to the tramlines.

Further Reform Acts in 1867 and 1884 gave all men over 21 the right to vote and to do so by secret ballot. (Women did not

Arthur James Balfour (1848–1930) was born of a wealthy family. He became a Conservative Member of Parliament in 1874 and Prime Minister in 1902. Though an eminent British statesman, he was much disliked by many Scots.

get the right to vote until 1918. They were supposed to busy themselves with their homes and children.)

When all men had the right to vote they took a keen interest in politics and argued about the merits and speeches of the Conservative leader, Benjamin Disraeli, and the Liberal leader, William Gladstone. Both the Conservative and Liberal parties were responsible for Acts that improved conditions for the poor.

The Trade Unions flourished in the 1870s and many educated working men discussed how the working classes could form their own party. This was done in 1893 under the leadership of Keir Hardie; by 1906 there were 29 members of the Independent Labour Party in Parliament.

There were 24 'Lib-Labs' as well, who supported both Liberal and Labour views. Between 1906 and 1911 a great number of new Acts of Parliament changed life enormously for industrial workers and their families.

When a Liberal government's reforms gave Old Age Pensions, Unemployment Pay and Sickness Benefits, they lifted a cloud of misery from many people's lives.

'Last Tram to Maryhill', a humorous sketch by Harvey Lambeth. In 1909 Glasgow's electrified tram cars carried 226 948 290 passengers.

A variety of fashionable 'Sunday' clothes.

James Keir Hardie (1856–1915) was selling newspapers in Lanarkshire at the age of 7 and working in the mines at 10. He educated himself at night school. He formed a Labour Party in 1888 and became a Member of Parliament in 1892.

David Stow's 'Uncovered School Room' in 1826. Children used maypoles, skipping ropes, garden tools and building materials for some activities. Stow spread his radical ideas on education through a demonstration school and the first teacher training college, but they spread slowly.

One famous Act of Parliament was the Education Act of 1872 which set up Board Schools for all children between 5 and 13.

Before 1872 there were simply not enough schools. In the 1860s one-sixth of Scottish children had no chance of getting to school at all: in Glasgow the figure was higher – 50%. Magistrates, ministers and businessmen worried about the terrible ignorance they saw round them. Sheriff Watson started 'Ragged Schools' for the poor in Aberdeen in 1841 and Dr. Guthrie did the same in Edinburgh in 1847. David Stow of Glasgow went even further and after starting a Sunday School and a day school he set up the first Training College for Teachers in the whole of Britain.

The new schools of 1872 were known as 'Board Schools' because they were built by School Boards (committees) elected by the ratepayers.

Board Schools gave keen pupils the chance of moving into trades and professions that called for a high level of education. At first, Board Schools concentrated on little more than the '3 Rs' but by 1892 they had won the right to present pupils for the new Leaving Certificate, first set up in 1887.

This called for a good knowledge of subjects such as English, Arithmetic, Mathematics, French, German, Latin, Greek and, later, Science. Those who passed might go to a university or college or train for some professional post. By 1892, also, girls were allowed to attend universities in Scotland and to take degrees.

The school-leaving age was raised to 14 in 1883 but until 1901 many children left

The University of Glasgow, founded in 1451, moved from Rotten Row (see the illustration on page 70) to the High Street in 1561 (see the illustration on page 125) and, three centuries later in 1870, to an impressive new building at Gilmorehill.

early. They could leave as soon as they had worked their way from Standard I to Standard V, and they could study part time only if they had passed Standard III. The examinations were held at the end of each year and a pupil had to pass the Standard examination before going into a higher class.

Many left early because they were poor and because the work they were going to do did not call for book knowledge. Even today nearly 80% of Scottish workers are employed in manual occupations (skilled, semi-skilled and unskilled). In the nineteenth century the percentage was even higher.

The school 'lines' at Hamilton board school in 1900. Many children went barefoot to school in summer but wore boots in winter – some went barefoot all the time.

27 Late Nineteenth Century: TIME OFF

Local fairs had provided entertainment since the Middle Ages, both in town and country. The sketch of Glasgow Fair in 1825 shows the kind of occasion that people enjoyed in the days before the coming of cinemas, radio and television. Peep-shows, theatres, acrobats, circuses, menageries and prize fights drew people to local fairgrounds. Many burghs had

Detail from the same picture of Glasgow Fair 1825 as on page 115. There were very few theatres because the Kirk disapproved of them – but music hall was to become popular later.

Cockfighting was popular till 1849 when it was banned (and later in some places). Teachers ran cockfights and kept the dead birds for food.

regular race-meetings as well. The 'Fair Fortnights' are still taken as local holidays today.

As early as 1770 fashionable people began to copy George III's visits to the seaside and Helensburgh was built as a resort for the wealthy. Largs, Dunoon and Rothesay grew up in the same way. Railways and steamboats opened up the whole Clyde area for holidays.

As life became easier for most people – working hours were cut and Saturday afternoon became a regular half holiday – townsfolk followed the example of the rich and flocked to enjoy the seaside and the country. Glaswegians went 'doon the watter' to seaside resorts on the Clyde. Edinburgh people made Portobello a favourite resort and each fishing village attracted holiday-makers.

Golf was the first game to be organised on a national basis. The Royal and Ancient Club of St. Andrews had laid down the rules in 1754 and the first Open Championship was held in 1860. Football followed, when the Scottish Football Association was founded in 1873. Queen's Park won the first Scottish Cup.

The first football clubs were all amateur but by the end of the century many teams used professional players. All the clubs attracted eager local support. Glasgow Rangers was started in 1872, playing on Glasgow Green, and its famous rival, Celtic, in 1883.

Village sports had always been popular – quoits, bowling and curling as well as football. Now they all became organised in national leagues, with away and home

Members of the Royal and Ancient Golf Club of St. Andrews about 1907. Some form of golf had been popular since the Middle Ages (see page 50) when, however, the ground was all rough.

The 'Ben More' leaving the Broomielaw, Glasgow, to sail 'doon the watter' to one of the Clydeside resorts, such as Dunoon. Dress on these occasions was still very formal.

Celtic playing Rangers in the final of the Glasgow Cup at Cathkin Park, Glasgow, on 26 May 1895. Celtic won. It was evidently too expensive for many people to buy tickets for the covered seats.

matches and competitions. Large crowds began to follow national contests and to travel to see their favourite teams play.

Cycling became a popular sport and pastime with the invention of the 'safety bicycle'. People began to see their own country for the first time. Amongst other things, people cycled to sports meetings and to the Highland Games which became very popular after Queen Victoria and Prince Albert attended the Braemar Gathering in the '50s.

The first Scottish motor-car, the Arrol-Johnston, built in 1895. Its top speed on the flat was 17 mph and Johnston was fined for speeding. Compare with Slezer's carriage scene (p. 83).

28 Late Nineteenth Century:
LIFE FOR THE WELL-TO-DO

Rich people had begun moving out of dirty city centres just after the middle of the eighteenth century.

Some built mansions in the country – sometimes on the grandest scale – copying the great houses of the nobility such as Hopetoun House. Others built smaller houses, the size according to their wealth. It took armies of servants to run all the houses but wages were low and there was never any shortage of butlers, footmen and maids.

Rich Dundee businessmen lived in Newport, across the Tay, and travelled by ferry between home and work. Aber-

deen had its select residential area in the precincts of the old college and Edinburgh its New Town. From Glasgow new suburbs expanded south and west.

Fine villas were built in the outer suburbs of cities. Fanciful 'Gothic' styles appeared which often sprouted pinnacles, turrets and spires. They were, however, beginning to offer their owners real comfort. Kitchens had coal-burning ranges with ovens, hot plates and water heaters. Some upper-class homes had gas cookers as early as the 1850s and gas lighting was common.

The better houses had baths and bath-

'Gothic' villa at Wemyss Bay, Firth of Clyde.

Sportsmen of the 1880s, stalking deer.

Sir Walter Scott (an Edinburgh lawyer) did much enthusiastic research into old tales, particularly those of the border country. In Scotland his poems and novels aroused new interest in national history – and all over Europe his stories and descriptions of natural scenery influenced the writing of novels. His first (verse) stories included 'The Lay of the Last Minstrel', 'Marmion' and 'The Lady of the Lake' and were followed by a series of novels beginning with 'Waverley' in 1814.

rooms though portable tubs and basins were more usual until the twentieth century. It was cleanliness that often marked off the well-to-do from the poor. 'Cleanliness is next to Godliness' was a favourite saying as preachers, teachers and politicians encouraged the working classes to model themselves on the 'upper' classes. Many people were convinced that if everyone worked hard, saved money and kept clean the whole country would be free of misery and disorder.

Walter Scott's poems and novels had given his readers a new and romantic view of Scotland and Scottish history. Travellers flocked to see the rugged highlands and picturesque glens.

When Queen Victoria and Prince Albert built a 'romantic' castle at Balmoral in 1855 landowners copied their example and built mansions in the Scottish Baronial style. When Albert designed his own tartan they took to wearing kilts, also.

Many highland estates became the playgrounds of the very rich. Stocked with deer, they catered for shooting parties from the south of Scotland and from England which came in search of deer and grouse among the deserted moors and mountains.

Clan chiefs and their sons no longer had any power. They were 'respectable landed gentry', often educated at English public schools.

The Broomielaw, Glasgow, in the 1880s. Traffic was still horse-drawn, lighting was by gas. Glasgow was a thriving city with a growing population – many of whom still lived in poverty among the city slums.

29 POSTSCRIPT TO THE NINETEENTH CENTURY

In the two hundred years that had passed since John Slezer published his drawings, Scotland had become a country of town dwellers. Seventy-five per cent of the population of 4½ million now lived in towns and large villages: of these, 1½ million lived in the five big cities – Glasgow, Edinburgh, Dundee, Aberdeen and Paisley.

Certainly the last years of the nineteenth century showed that the Industrial Revolution could bring a better way of life for rich and poor alike. Britain grew steadily richer because of her industrial exports and her great empire which stretched over a quarter of the globe. She was involved in few wars.

Steam, gas and electricity made possible all sorts of labour-saving appliances which helped to make lives easier and more varied. The nineteenth-century way of life continued until 1914, when World War I broke out. Motor cars and telephones had certainly appeared in the nineteenth century and the first aeroplane flew in 1903, but the impact of these inventions came after 1914.

30 A GLANCE AT THE TWENTIETH CENTURY

The twentieth century has been so packed with changes that it needs a whole book to itself.

Like the rest of the people of Britain, Scots were badly affected by the two World Wars and by the slump in industry that came between them. Scots were, in fact, hit hardest as so many worked in the heavy industries. At one time 400 000 people were out of work, 30 % of the total labour force.

Since then governments have worked to provide each area with a wide range of light industries so that if one factory closes its workers can find jobs nearby.

One of the most promising solutions to the problems of working and housing has been the building of New Towns such as Glenrothes, Cumbernauld, Livingston, East Kilbride and Irvine.

They are specially planned to provide a variety of work (for both men and women) and housing suitable for different sizes and sorts of families. Each New Town has its own transport services and links with main highways and airports. It contains all the amenities of a town: shops, churches, libraries, cinemas, community halls, hospitals, restaurants, cafés, public houses, parks, playing fields and open spaces.

Electricity (here cleanly produced by the power of water falling over the dam at Pitlochry) has completely changed conditions.

The original apparatus used in the 1920s by John Logie Baird, the pioneer of television.

*Aerial view of houses at Livingston New Town. ►
Authorities provide a variety of sizes and styles to suit different needs – one-storey and two-storey houses, small (five-storey) blocks of flats.*

An American cargo 'plane at Prestwick airport, the most important international airport in the country. The speedy transport of goods and passengers between towns and countries would have astonished people of even a century ago – as would the speed with which news is transmitted from the other side of the world by telephone, wireless and television.

If their industries prosper and if they can re-create a genuine sense of community, New Towns may provide the best plan for living in the Scotland of the future.

In the meantime, authorities are faced with problems whose roots lie deep in history. One of the problems arises from the way that the population is grouped. For two hundred years people have drifted into the central lowland belt in search of work so that now the majority of people are crammed into one portion of the land.

This concentration of people in one area has made the cities full of old and over-crowded houses. Many of the industries that attracted people to the cities no longer exist.

It is always unwise to predict what will happen in the future. The discovery of oil off the Scottish coast, the entry of Britain into the European Common Market and the re-zoning of local government all suggest possible developments.

Scots are better equipped technologically to satisfy their wants than any of their ancestors. The future depends on how well they use the skills and knowledge inherited from the past.

Trays of scampi being brought ashore at Oban. They would perhaps be recognised today by the 'strand loopers' of the Middle Stone Age.

Books

Barclay, J. B.: Edinburgh from Earliest Times to the Present Day *Black* 1965
Boog-Watson, E. J.: An 18th Century Highlander *Oxford University Press* 1965
Cameron, A. D.: History for Young Scots, Volumes I & II *Oliver & Boyd* 1963
            Living in Scotland 1760–1820 *Oliver & Boyd* 1969
Fidler, K.: Flodden Field *Lutterworth* 1971
       The '45: Culloden *Lutterworth* 1973
Junior Reference Books *Black*
  Allen, E.: Victorian Children
  Baker, M.: Food and Cooking
  Hoare, R. J.: The Story of Aircraft
  Leighton, P.: Coins and Tokens
  Manning, R.: Heraldry
  Unstead, R. J.: Castles
          Monasteries
          Travel by Road
  White, P.: Fairs and Circuses
  Wilkinson, F.: Arms and Armour
Kyle, E.: Queen of Scots *Nelson* 1957
Lobban, R. D.: The Clansmen *Oxford University Press* 1969
Macphail, I. M. M.: A History of Scotland for Schools, Books 1 & 2 *Arnold* 1954
Miller, M. J.: King Robert the Bruce *Macdonald* 1970
Nichol, N.: Glasgow from Earliest Times to the Present Day *Black* 1969
Nichol, N.: 16th Century Flashbacks *Oliver & Boyd* 1973
  The Barton Brothers, Scottish Sea Captains
  John Cowan, Scottish Burgess
  Thomas Crawford, Scottish Gentleman
  Sir Duncan Campbell, Highland Laird
Oliver, J.: The Young Robert Bruce *Parrish* 1962
Peach, L. Du Garde: Robert the Bruce *Ladybird Books* 1964
Plaidy, J.: The Young Mary Queen of Scots *Parrish* 1962
Raine, M.: Culloden *Wheaton* 1967
Scarfe, G.: A Highland Glen About 250 Years Ago *Longman* 1967
Scott, T.: Tales of King Robert the Bruce *Pergamon* 1969
Sinclair, N. F.: Living History of Scotland *Holmes McDougall* 1970
Then and There series *Longman*
  Brash, R.: Glasgow in the Tramway Age, 1968
  McKechnie, K.: A Border Woollen Town in the Industrial Revolution, 1968

continued overleaf

Nichol, N.: Glasgow and the Tobacco Lords, 1966
Ritchie, W. K.: Scotland in the Time of Wallace and Bruce, 1970
Ritchie, W. K.: Edinburgh in its Golden Age, 1967
Shapiro, H.: Scotland in the Days of James VI, 1970
Shapiro, H.: Scotland in the Days of Burns, 1968
Stevenson, W.: The Days of James IV of Scotland, 1964
Stevenson, W.: The Jacobite Rising of 1745, 1968
Thomson, O.: The Romans in Scotland, 1968

For visual material
History at Source: Scotland: The Rise of Cities 1694–1905
        Scotland: Revolution in Industry 1703–1913 } *Evans*

Aerial view of Grangemouth oil refinery and chemicals plant.

Museums

Readers would be well advised to explore the possibilities of museums, libraries and art galleries in their area (many of which are not well publicised). Towns in the following list certainly have one or more and many will have castles and mansions nearby which may be of interest.

Aberdeen	Elgin	Largs
Airdrie	Falkirk	Lerwick
Alloway	Forfar	Meigle
Annan	Forres	Melrose
Anstruther	Fort George	Millport
Arbroath	Fort William	Milngavie
Auchindrain	Glamis	Montrose
Ayr	Glasgow	Nairn
Banff	Glencoe	Newtonmore
Biggar	Glenesk	North Berwick
Blair Atholl	Greenock	Paisley
Blantyre	Hamilton	Peebles
Brechin	Hawick	Perth
Bruar Falls	Inverkeithing	Peterhead
Buckie	Inverness	Rothesay
Campbeltown	Inverurie	St. Andrews
Castle Douglas	Jedburgh	Saltcoats
Ceres	Kilbarchan	Selkirk
Coldstream	Kilmarnock	South Queensferry
Cromarty	Kingussie	Stirling
Culross	Kinnesswood	Stranraer
Dalry	Kinross	Strathaven
Dumfries	Kirkcaldy	Stromness
Dunblane	Kirkcudbright	Tain
Dundee	Kirkintilloch	Thurso
Dunfermline	Kirkoswald	Withorn
Ecclefechan	Kirkwall	Wick
Edinburgh	Kirriemuir	

Index

Acknowledgements

The author and publisher would like to thank the following individuals and organisations for permission to reproduce their pictures in this book:

Aberdeen Public Libraries 105a, 107c, 144a, 150b

Aberdeen University Library 136a, 155c

Aerofilms 1, 159c

Airdrie Public Library 148a

Earl of Ancaster 82

Banff, Royal Burgh of 15b

B. T. Batsford Ltd 75a

Birmingham Museum & Art Gallery 124b

Bodleian Library 93a

British Airports Authority 160a

British Museum, Trustees of 36b, 48a & b, 49a, 54, 56a, 61b, 68a, 78a, 90a, 94, 96a, 109c, 123a

British Petroleum facing p. 160

British Waterways Board 138

Vincent Brown 67b

Cambridge, University of, Committee for Aerial Photography 22b, 50b

Sir John Clerk of Penicuik Bt 84a

Corpus Christi College, Cambridge, Master and Fellows of 67a

Crown Copyright: Department of the Environment 4a, b & c, 6a & b, 7, 9a & b, 18b, 20a, 23, 25b, 31b, 36a, 37c, 41a, 43b, 44a, 45a, 46a, 51, 52, 57, 58a, 63c, 70b

Crown Copyright: Royal Commission on Ancient Monuments, Scotland: title page, foreword page 56b, 62a & b, 63a & b, 65b, 87c, 91b, 95a, 106a

Cumbernauld Development Corporation 139c

Dumfries Burgh Museum 111a & b

Edinburgh City Libraries 85c, 87b, 139b, 140b, 143a, 155b, 157b

Edinburgh, University of 144c

Ferranti Ltd 122a

Galashiels, Burgh of 75b

Glasgow Art Gallery 113

Glasgow Museum of Transport 156

A. R. B. Haldane from *Drove Roads of Scotland* published by David & Charles 99a, b & c

Director, Hamilton Burgh Museum 153b

Huntly House Museum, Edinburgh 110c

Jarrold Colour Publications 87d, 93c, 145a

Livingstone Memorial, Blantyre 141b & c

Mansell Collection: first contents page, 58b, 60a & b, 89b, 93b, 126, 131, 134b, 137a, 142c, 143b, 147a, 149a, 150c, 154b

Ivan D. Margary, from *Roman Roads in Britain* published by John Baker: half-title page

Mary Evans Picture Library 123c, 136c, 147b

Merchants' House of Glasgow 77a

Mitchell Library, Glasgow 89c, 108a, 124a, 125c, 130a, 131a, 133b, 139a, 142a & d, 148b, 149b, 150a, 152, 153a, 155a, 157a

National Army Museum 92b

National Coal Board of Scotland 135b, d & e

National Galleries of Scotland 68b, 71c, 78b, 79a & b, 86, 88a & b, 97a & b, 98a, 103c, 104a & c, 107b, 115a, 117a & b, 119a, 121a, b & c, 123b & e, 127a, 137b, 144b, 157c

National Library of Scotland 71a & b, 73a & b, 80a & b, 98b, 101a & b, 102, 103a & b, 105b, 112a, b & c, 116b, 117d, 120a, 121d, 133a, 134a

National Maritime Museum 142b

National Museum of Antiquities of Scotland 2a & c, 3b & c, 5a & b, 8a, b, c & d, 9c, 10b, 11a & b, 16a & d, 21a & b, 22a, c, d & e, 26a & b, 29b, 37a, 38b, 49b & c, 53a & b, 55a & b, 66a & c, 68c, 72a & b, 73c, 80c, 91c & d, 92a, 96b, 114a & b, 135a

National Museum of Denmark 15a

National Museum of Wales 14a

National Portrait Gallery 151a

National Trust for Scotland 76, 136b, 146b

Sir David Ogilvy Bt 77b

Old Glasgow Museum, Glasgow Green 10a, 20b, 145b, 146a

Peter Baker Photography 159a, 160b

Phaidon Press 41b

Post Office Records 128, 129b & c

Radio Times Hulton Picture Library 37b, 74, 100, 108b & c, 119b, 127b, 129d, 130b, 137c, 158

Reading, University of, Museum of English Rural Life 132b

Kenneth Robinson 107a

Duke of Roxburghe 42

Royal Norwegian Ministry of Foreign Affairs 39